D1553243

THE LOST
ISLAND

Opteekninge van t eylandt *Amsterdam*,

't Eylandt Amsterdam gelegen ten noorden Ongeraed 12 a 12 mijl
van t Eylandt St pauler betoont dat alsic gepe ten Oosten in dese voorschre
't figuude voor Aangehoulden

1. Eijlandt Amsterdam

nº 1.

A

Betoont Alsoo oost ende digt onder Doevoet is
Omtrent 6 loden Ter sijde Clip Alsbe A:

2 Eijlandt Amsterdam

nº 2.

Betoont Alsoo d top de hoogte 2275 van dese hoe toen Alsoo
dan d west sijd Alsie van 1 vaam Swart Crugel gemt

3 Eijlandt Amsterdam

nº 3.

noorden: Als ic 4 mijle van dese betoont alsic

THE LOST ISLAND

ALONE AMONG THE FRUITFUL

AND MULTIPLYING

Alfred van Cleef

Translated by S. J. Leinbach

Metropolitan Books

Henry Holt and Company

New York

Metropolitan Books
Henry Holt and Company, LLC
Publishers since 1866
115 West 18th Street
New York, New York 10011

Metropolitan Books™ is a registered
trademark of Henry Holt and Company, LLC.

Originally published in The Netherlands in 1999
under the title *Het verdwaalde eiland*, by Meulenhoff, Amsterdam.

Library of Congress Cataloging-in-Publication Data

Cleef, Alfred van, date.
    [Verdwaalde eiland English]
    The lost island : alone among the fruitful and multiplying / by Alfred van Cleef;
translated by S. J. Leinbach.—1st American ed.
        p.   cm.
    Originally published: Het verdwaalde eiland. Amsterdam : Meulenhoff, 1999.
    Includes bibliographical references.
    ISBN 0-8050-7225-X
    1. Amsterdam Island (Terres australes et antarctiques françaises)   2. Cleef,
Alfred van, 1954—Travel—Terres australes et antarctiques françaises—Amsterdam
Island.   I. Title.

DS349.9.A57C5413   2004
916.9'9—dc22   2004040322

First American Edition 2004

Designed by Michelle McMillian

Printed in the United States of America

1   3   5   7   9   10   8   6   4   2

Hebban olla vogala
Nestas hagunnan
Hinase hic enda thu

The birds have all
Begun their nests
Except for you and me

—OLDEST SURVIVING DUTCH TEXT,
ELEVENTH CENTURY

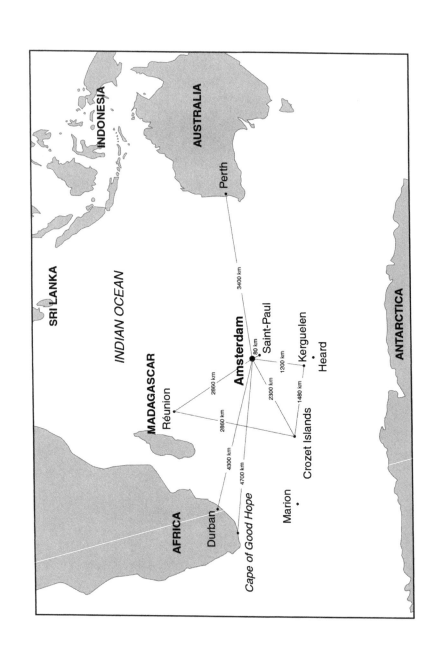

INDONESIA

AUSTRALIA

• Perth

SRI LANKA

INDIAN OCEAN

3400 km

MADAGASCAR
Réunion

Amsterdam

Saint-Paul

• 80 km

Kerguelen

Heard

1200 km

2860 km

2300 km

1480 km

2860 km

Crozet Islands

ANTARCTICA

4300 km

4700 km

AFRICA

Durban

Cape of Good Hope

Marion •

THE LOST
ISLAND

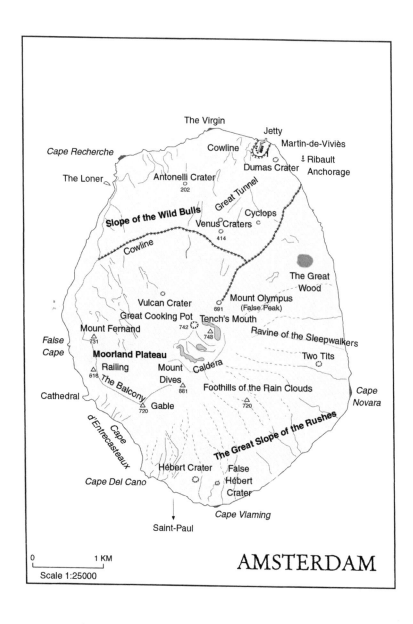

The Virgin

Jetty

Cape Recherche

Cowline

Martin-de-Viviès

‡ Ribault

The Loner

Antonelli Crater

Dumas Crater

Anchorage

202

Great Tunnel

Slope of the Wild Bulls

Cyclops

Venus Craters

Cowline

414

The Great
Wood

Vulcan Crater

Mount Olympus

(False Peak)

Great Cooking Pot

Tench's Mouth

691

Mount Fernand

742

748

Ravine of the Sleepwalkers

False
Cape

731

Moorland Plateau

Mount

Caldera

Two Tits

Railing

Dives

616

The Balcony

881

Foothills of the Rain Clouds

Cape
Novara

Cathedral

720

Gable

720

Cape
d'Entrecasteaux

The Great Slope of the Rushes

Hébert Crater

False

Cape Del Cano

Hébert
Crater

Saint-Paul

Cape Vlaming

0   1 KM

AMSTERDAM

Scale 1:25000

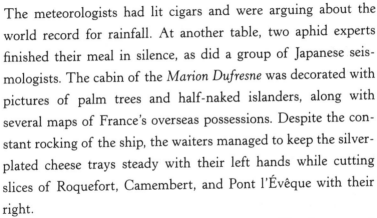

The meteorologists had lit cigars and were arguing about the world record for rainfall. At another table, two aphid experts finished their meal in silence, as did a group of Japanese seismologists. The cabin of the *Marion Dufresne* was decorated with pictures of palm trees and half-naked islanders, along with several maps of France's overseas possessions. Despite the constant rocking of the ship, the waiters managed to keep the silver-plated cheese trays steady with their left hands while cutting slices of Roquefort, Camembert, and Pont l'Évêque with their right.

The social divisions on board were very clear. The cleaners and stokers were black, as were the day laborers who ferried in from Madagascar: They were kept out of sight, and took their meals belowdecks. Meanwhile the ship's officers and the nearly one hundred passengers enjoyed their four-course afternoon and evening meals in the spacious dining room, which was furnished in a tasteful, modern style.

The uniformed crew members—military draftees, mechanics,

and maintenance workers—were the first to be served, though the white-liveried waiters were quick to snatch their plates before the speakers blared: "Second seating for the afternoon meal. Second seating, *bon appétit.*" This was the cue for those whose rank or seniority placed them among the most important passengers—the higher-ranking officers and the scientists. Evidently the *maître d'* had been informed I was an official guest of the ministry, since he greeted me by name—a courtesy otherwise reserved only for the captain and the *administrateur supérieur.*

From the dining room I looked out over the water. The sea was calm. We had been underway for some time, but it took much longer than I thought before the harbor of Saint-Denis faded completely from view.

We had each boarded separately, having said good-bye to our loved ones, who knew we were headed for the ends of the earth. When it was my turn to climb up the gangplank, I was welcomed by the secretary-general, who immediately grabbed me by the arm to introduce me to the administrateur. I had known the man would be sailing with us; still, it was a shock to actually see him in the flesh. I held out my hand as he climbed on deck. He gave it a quick shake and went on his way without so much as glancing at me.

This was the culmination of a struggle that had dragged on for years, which I appeared to have won; but I felt no sense of triumph, just a hollow wariness that, although I'd come farther than I ever dared hope, I had yet to reach my final destination. I assumed the administrateur would continue to do everything in his power to thwart my plans. Nevertheless, I now felt no one could stop me, that I would set my foot on that far-flung lost island and stay there, perched in the middle of the empty sea, when the administrateur would sail back to the *Marion Dufresne*'s home port at Réunion, over the horizon.

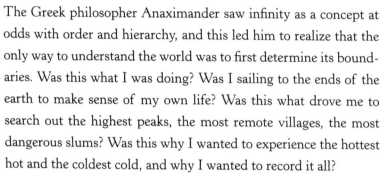

The Greek philosopher Anaximander saw infinity as a concept at odds with order and hierarchy, and this led him to realize that the only way to understand the world was to first determine its boundaries. Was this what I was doing? Was I sailing to the ends of the earth to make sense of my own life? Was this what drove me to search out the highest peaks, the most remote villages, the most dangerous slums? Was this why I wanted to experience the hottest hot and the coldest cold, and why I wanted to record it all?

At night I would switch on my illuminated globe and they would appear—mysterious dots, far removed from any land, little black specks with names like Ascension and Ailinglapalap, Henderson and Mokil—floating in the middle of the ocean as if they'd been torn from their moorings and set adrift, abandoned to the elements. And out of all these isolated places, I was seeking the most extreme.

My eyes first fell on Bouvet Island, southwest of the Cape of Good Hope, and just past the northern limit of the Antarctic drift-ice. It had been discovered in the early eighteenth century by the French explorer Jean-Baptiste Charles Bouvet de Lozier, who struggled for ten days to come ashore before finally giving up. Peering through the fog, Bouvet was just able to discern a group of snow-covered rocks—and was immediately convinced he had discovered no mere island, but a promontory of the long-sought Terra Australis Incognita, the fabled last continent, a new land where "the torch of the Gospel" could be spread to the greater honor and glory of the king of France. This dream dissolved some fifty years later, when James Cook proved that Terra Australis was nothing more than a cartographic fantasy, and the tiny island was lost for another two centuries before anyone rediscovered what was arguably the most inhospitable, foggy, icy, and infertile spot on Earth. A patch of rock so forlorn that not even the British protested when one day a group of whalers finally planted the Norwegian flag on it.

Extreme as Bouvet was, it wasn't quite extreme enough. Although *The Guinness Book of World Records* called the place "the remotest island on Earth," I considered that a fraud since it was too close to the nearest landmass. So in the end I decided against Bouvet.

Saint Helena and Tristan da Cunha are without question two of the world's most famous isolated islands, but there are clearly others in the Pacific even more remote. And while the Marquesas Islands are about as far from any continent as you can find, that part of the Pacific is littered with archipelagoes—so they, too, were out.

I eventually discovered what I was looking for in the southern Indian Ocean. Nowhere else was the sea more bare; nowhere were the waves higher or the winds more fierce. And perched in the middle of this wild mass of water, equally far from Sri Lanka and

South Africa, Australia and Antarctica, nearly two thousand miles from the closest continent, was a minuscule volcanic peak. There was no longer any doubt. I had fallen under the spell of a place surrounded by endlessness, the most far-flung island on the planet, where even the name seemed linked to my fate: Amsterdam.

The island of my dreams turned out to belong to France. Politically it is part of the French Southern and Antarctic Lands, which are governed by an administrateur supérieur appointed by the president in Paris. These territories comprise an all but imaginary realm that consists of a few volcanic peaks scattered thousands of miles apart, across a section of ocean the size of Western Europe: the Crozet Archipelago, the Kerguelen Islands, Saint-Paul, and Amsterdam. Another district, known as Terre Adélie, lies on the Antarctic continent; according to the advertisements it is "larger than continental France"—at least in winter—although in truth it isn't much more than an empty mass of ice.

Amsterdam has no airport and no harbor. A helicopter taking off in the inhabited world would never be able to reach it. The only way there is aboard the *Marion Dufresne,* the last surviving French mail boat, which, besides carrying mailbags and provisions for the southern islands, is equipped with a helicopter and a number of life rafts and dinghies, which are manned by Malagasies. Based in Réunion, the ship courses among the French islands, stopping at Amsterdam a few times a year, but to make the journey you need to have a special invitation.

The island has no permanent inhabitants, only temporary residents—meteorologists and other scientists who never stay longer than a year and a half at a stint. And this no-man's-land has been even less hospitable to women: Not one ever spent more than two days there in the course of the past century.

Amsterdam met all my demands. The island was remote to the point of being inaccessible; it was barely inhabited, although supplied with meat and wine; it was small enough to be taken in at a glance, but not without a variety of features. I could already see myself on top of the highest peak, gazing into the distance in all directions. There, high over Amsterdam, I would once again find happiness—and this belief was more than simple hope. It was my stubborn resolution, a personal manifesto.

Doubting that any French bureaucrat would be swayed by mere personal obsession, I wrote a letter to the administrateur requesting permission to follow in the footsteps of the Dutch East India Captain Willem Hesselsz. de Vlamingh, the first person to actually set foot on the island—some three hundred years earlier. I wrote that I would need at least a month for my research, though I was prepared to extend my stay for up to four months or half a year if the island's virtual inaccessibility left me no other choice.

Two months later I received a reply: cordial thanks for my letter, which had been duly received. Unfortunately the official Year of the Ocean had so disrupted the scheduled service to the Southern Provinces—which was minimal at best—that I was asked to write back in three years. The letter was signed "Respectfully yours" by one Madame Marie-Thérèse Clément, for the secretary-general, on behalf of the administrateur supérieur.

The prospect of having to wait so long did not dampen my enthusiasm. In fact, the opposite happened: I could feel my connection with Amsterdam growing from mere fascination into a full-fledged passion, a compulsion, a physical necessity. I was not about to give up; I was determined to pursue my goal as fervently as I had run after certain women I had broken up with and desperately wanted back. I wanted to overcome the sense I was adrift in life—and this was why I embraced Amsterdam as my very own, for now and forever.

Three years later I wrote another letter to the administrateur. This time I chose to proceed more cautiously, having been advised, by someone with personal experience, of a Gallic cultural "sensitivity to hierarchy." So I decided first to approach the director of the Institut Français in Amsterdam, via a mutual acquaintance. This man studied my "case," and at the end of December forwarded it to the scientific attaché at the French Embassy in The Hague, who in turn passed it on to the proper authorities, as he assured me, with a personal recommendation. The attaché also told me that all persons applying to stay on Amsterdam had to go through a rigorous selection process, as life on the island demanded exceptional social skills.

Although the attaché had told me a reply would not be long in coming, months passed with no answer, and at the beginning of March, I decided that the time had come to plead my case personally in Paris.

The rue des Renaudes was a long but unremarkable street not far from the place Charles de Gaulle, in the seventeenth *arrondissement*. Situated between a realtor's office and "Ed l'Épicier" was a building with a tall, narrow front that seemed more focused on itself than open to the outside world. By the door was a modest yet distinguished plaque that read *Territoire des Terres Australes et Antarctiques Françaises*. I pressed the gold-colored bell. The doorman showed me in to a dark-brown paneled anteroom, where I waited for Madame Clément, who managed the office, while she traveled in a teakwood elevator from the fifth floor down to the first. The room had three glass display cases with philatelic exhibits from the Southern and Antarctic Lands, and key rings in the shape of penguins. I looked at a building directory, which matched the departments of Sovereignty Affairs, Research, and Logistics to the proper floors and listed the rooms of the departmental secretariats and various branches. A series of photographs adorned the walls: bearded men in fur hats; ships against backdrops of icebergs and winter-blue oceans.

Madame Clément was wearing a suit, which made her look older than her years. She was charming but stiff, and didn't seem the least bit interested in the fact that a man from Amsterdam, Holland, wanted to spend time on Amsterdam Island. My request to be granted an extended stay was out of the question, she informed me; no outsider had ever stayed on the island. "But your petition was forwarded, and I am acquainted with what you wish to accomplish," she said, pointing to a folder labeled VAN CLEEF that she had laid on the table. She handed me a brochure with a picture of penguins on the cover. It was all about the Southern Territories: surface area, administrative organization, flora, scientific research, climate, algae extraction. Without asking me anything else, she turned on a video, and a man in an orange raincoat appeared on the large screen, who proceeded to explain how a herd of wild cattle came to be on Amsterdam Island. A storm was raging in the background. The sound quality was poor to begin with, and Madame Clément kept talking over the film. "I wanted to show you this to give you an impression of what it's like."

I began to talk her around by pointing out the unique ties between the two Amsterdams. By researching the traces of Willem de Vlamingh, I argued, I could make an important contribution to the historiography of the Dutch East India Company. Not only did I want to visit the island, I wanted to *understand* it, and this meant I needed to experience its silence, isolation, and seclusion.

"It's a closed community," replied Madame Clément. "Your presence could cause some tension." She took out the sailing schedule for the *Marion Dufresne* and highlighted with a yellow marker a box labeled AMS. "There are two crossings during the southern summer. The ship sails out of Réunion and puts in at the Crozet Islands and Kerguelen before reaching Amsterdam—that's three weeks. The return trip takes a week. Depending on the weather, of course. If you left in December, you could spend a month on Amsterdam and be back by the end of January." She smiled. "But it's all up to you, except for the permission, of course—that's for others to decide. Although it's unclear at the moment exactly who. The administrateur supérieur has just retired, and even though his successor has been appointed, he still hasn't taken office."

She asked for the secretary-general, a Mediterranean-looking man who made an aloof impression as he strode over to me, cast a tense glance at his watch, and said, "You have to realize that Amsterdam is nothing more than a meteorological station and a scientific base, with a minimum of comforts. No one there has time for you." He went on to say that, ever since 1950, when the French established a permanent presence on the island, no one who had applied without an official invitation had ever been granted permission to stay. The fact that I wasn't even French further complicated the matter. When I mentioned that Amsterdam Island was French territory, and that France belonged to the European Union, he conceded that I had a point. But my request was unusual, and the Administration of the Southern Lands was grappling with more important issues: The new administrateur had been charged with introducing some difficult reforms and extensive budget cuts. "But what do I care," the secretary suddenly blurted out. "I only wish to repeat that the island is wild and inaccessible: There really is nothing to see. Still, as far as I'm concerned, you can stay for a month. Provided you're prepared to cover your own expenses, and I can tell you: It won't be cheap. In about six weeks I should know more."

It was going to happen. I was sure of it. The secretary-general stood up and shook my hand. In the doorway he turned around. "Of course you understand that the new administrateur will have to authorize this decision after he takes office, but that should be nothing more than a formality."

Amsterdam was almost exactly as small as Manhattan Island, but for me it was of massive importance; I considered it the crown jewel of geography. Sometimes you could even find the place on the tiny world maps that showed only a few cities per continent. My favorite was an inflatable plastic beach ball-globe—it had enough space for the name to be printed in large letters, especially since the surrounding area was so empty. Any good-sized globe could be rotated in such a way that India, Australia, and Africa were mere margins, insignificant borders around a vast expanse of blue, with the island Amsterdam as its undisputed center. But what I liked most of all were the atlases, where the tiny island held its own alongside the geographical giants—its position on the planet firmly established.

Sometimes the island was mislabeled as Nieuw or Nouvelle; I even had a Neu Amsterdam in my collection. As far as I was concerned that was inexcusable: Not only did the unadorned Amsterdam sound better—that is to say, more radical and more extreme—it was also the island's official name. I couldn't understand why my friends were so unfazed about such egregious inconsistencies when I pointed this out.

I, on the other hand, could easily reel off every species of petrel found on Amsterdam, or recite the average number of gale force winds to hit the island in a given year. I knew the names of all the ships that had run aground on its rocks. I also knew the exact mating season of the Indian yellow-nosed albatross, and the fact that it rained on the island two hundred twenty-three days of the year. I collected such facts and put them in folders running from A (Amsterdam Island in the 16th Century) to Z (Zooplankton).

Despite the secretary-general's promise, I had a growing sense that unseen powers were intent on foiling my project, since after granting me permission he never got back to me, and kept himself inaccessible. Three months had passed after my visit to Paris and I was none the wiser. I was at the mercy of administrators, secretaries, messengers, caught between prolonged absences and administrative complications, stuck in a world ruled by an elusive administrateur supérieur who had just taken office and had probably never laid eyes on the Van Cleef dossier.

Then, to my surprise, I discovered that the Dutch ambassador in Paris had agreed to take a personal interest in my application, so that my longing for the infinite expanses had now become a matter of state. The ambassador proved to be an old pro, who was reputed to be both a vain schemer and a first-rate diplomat who knew exactly how to handle all levels of dignitaries. He personally wrote to the administrateur and asked him to grant my request. The latter sent back an ominous reply:

As I have only recently assumed my office as chief administrator of the Southern Lands, before answering Monsieur Van Cleef I should first like to visit the territories myself, as I intend to do in mid-July. Incidentally, I must point out to you that no one outside the permanent staff has ever been allowed to stay on Amsterdam for more than two days, if for no other reason than the fact that the structural and organizational facilities are not designed to accommodate outsiders.

I tried to speak to the administrateur before he left on his official tour, but he was shielded in every possible way. I continued to call nearly every day, especially after the head of the logistics department accidentally let slip that the administrateur would be in for several days before leaving for the Southern Lands. By avoiding Madame Clément and taking advantage of one of her unsuspecting colleagues, I finally got the administrateur himself on the line. "The president of the Republic has charged me with moving our offices from Paris to Réunion. You understand that this matter has priority," he said in an affected tone of voice that would brook no contradiction. "As far as your petition is concerned: My letter to your ambassador is clear. I have nothing to add. I would now like to end this conversation."

Meanwhile I got back in touch with the scientific attaché to the French Embassy in The Hague. "You know, this administrateur might actually be a charming man who's extremely interested in your project," he said, "but he could just as easily be your classic French civil servant, and those aren't people you want to rub the wrong way. Incidentally, the person I spoke with in Paris sounded pretty pessimistic about your application. Just getting you there, for example, would require the use of a helicopter; and apparently the weather is an absolute nightmare."

The more people I told about my obsession with the island, the more I heard suggestions that the real reason the French government didn't want me on Amsterdam was because of some secret research. Maybe the island was a covert military base. Or a place of exile for scientists who'd lost their mind conducting nuclear or chemical experiments, and had been deported to avoid a national scandal. Perhaps they were even laboring under the delusion that they were performing important scientific research, while in reality they were inmates in the world's most remote psychiatric clinic.

Searching the Internet for possible clues, I found an alphabetical overview of local algae species, tables showing measurements of "atmospheric carbon dioxide," a graph of the average methane concentration, and a mysterious photograph of "conjoined orographic clouds" that had been observed on Amsterdam on February 6, 1951, and had been posted on a website of the Hungarian Meteorological Service. A physicist I spoke to about my plans seemed quite unimpressed by the results of my investigation: "That's just a lot of data collection—holding little flasks in the seawater and reading meters." The only thing that piqued his interest was the evidence of long-term magnetospheric research. "Now *that* could be military," he said. "Just think of Alaska. As we speak, the American army is working on a megaproject there to influence the solar wind as it hits the earth."

Then he mentioned something about submarine radar and biological and oceanographic experiments, but I couldn't understand what he was saying, and I didn't even ask what solar wind was.

I could tell something was about to happen, and it did. In September the Dutch ambassador received a letter from the administrateur overruling the secretary-general's decision to let me stay. The language was chilling:

After personally visiting the Southern Lands I can confirm that neither the structure of the permanent station nor its function is suited for admitting anyone not part of the mission, regardless of his personal qualities or nationality. Furthermore, for reasons of security, all persons wishing to conduct activities outside the base must at all times be supervised, so that the lack of available personnel alone makes it quite impossible for M. Van Cleef to stay on Amsterdam Island for any extended period.

He did suggest that I could take the cruise through the Southern Lands as a paying passenger, with the possibility of visiting Amsterdam for two days. But what I sought was isolation, and two days wasn't enough to find that, so I rejected the offer.

The ambassador let me know there was nothing more he could do for me; no doubt the administrateur had sent my petition straight to the file of rejected applications. I wished that I could do the same thing, that I could simply tear up my letters to the administrateur, shred my folders on the social behavior of Amsterdam fur seals, and dump all the material I had been amassing for months on the paleogeographic history of tectonic plates in the southern Indian Ocean. But I couldn't. In my whole life I had never slammed a single door.

And yet there was no going back. I felt I had torn down all the foundations and was merely drifting through life. My relationship with Saskia, one in a series after Eva, was over. I had quit my job at the liberal paper.

My father had always said to me, "It doesn't matter what you do, just make sure you never have a boss over you." I'd always taken that to mean I should strive to be master of my own fate, but the end result was that I kept everyone—including myself—at a distance, and found it difficult to give myself to anyone completely. Eva had been the only one I had chosen unconditionally; when she left me, I was paralyzed.

I had learned to live the life of the lonely, to the point where I could rattle off my favorite ready-made dinners (guinea fowl with stewed pears and chicken casserole). I was suffering from loneliness, but this was the inevitable consequence of my fear of losing control over my life.

I never let my lovers get any farther than my outermost walls. The spiritual German, the woman pursuing her degree in European studies, the television producer, the violinist—I had loved each of them, tenderly, but when they opened up, when they wanted to give more, I rejected them. Always with a smile, but nevertheless unyielding. I couldn't help it.

I kept my distance from my friends and their families. I only went to the beach when everyone else was leaving. I couldn't join in their conversations about baby carriages, skateboards, amusement parks, camping trips, and schools. In the city I was showered with birth announcements, which I usually answered with strained or even provocative replies, congratulating the parents on their "new spawn." I avoided anyone who smelled of nest, like the one writer friend I ran into on the street. "Second book?" I asked. "Second child," she replied, and pedaled on.

When my trip to Amsterdam Island looked more hopeless than ever, I could no longer control my darker urges, which suddenly began to get the upper hand.

I started smoking dope every day: As soon as I would wake up I'd buy a pre-rolled joint from the coffee shop on the corner. Then I'd trudge through the streets of the city, my head downcast, hoping I wouldn't run into anyone I knew. My bathroom mirror showed a pallid, pacing man. Dazed. Tense. Balding. I wished for gloomy weather and heavy rain. I was ashamed; I tried to forget what I wanted to forget. I clung to the idea of going to Amsterdam more stubbornly than ever, and the desire became a craving I refused to give up.

Soon it became an established ritual. First I would smoke a joint at home. Once my senses were sufficiently numb, I would drive out to the Beukenplein Square. Although no one could possibly know why I went there, I had the feeling that everyone was staring at my uncontrollable excitement—which is why I always took my car instead of biking. I would park and then sprint past the storefronts, pausing now and then to look around. If someone was headed my way, I would turn and look at a window display of poultry or tropical goods.

Then I would slip, unnoticed, into the De Beuk video store with its shuttered windows. The man behind the counter had greasy yellow hair and smelled of hand-rolled cigarettes. I rarely said a word to him. The store's clientele ranged from well-heeled men in nice suits to tattooed men with dogs, but there was never anyone who knew me. Still, I looked up every time the door opened. It was a good place. There were never any women, so I didn't have to feel ashamed. Once you were done with the material, you could drop it into a special slot in the middle of the night. The selection was good; I just didn't care for how it was organized. If I owned a video store with shuttered windows, I wouldn't open before sundown, and I'd make sure everything was arranged alphabetically by genre and not by production company. But I did not have a video store of my own, so I was completely at the mercy of De Beuk's proprietor: "You've already had this one."

. . .

After a few weeks I pulled myself together: If the administrateur thought he'd heard the last of Monsieur Van Cleef, he was wrong. Of course it was unrealistic to think I could still make the December sailing, and that was the only one that would allow me to spend a month on the island, at the peak of the southern summer, from the end of December to the end of January—plus four to five weeks at sea aboard the *Marion Dufresne*. During the rest of the year the ship only made the voyage once every four months. In any case, I had a whole year ahead of me. I decided to launch a major offensive, attacking the administrateur from all fronts while simultaneously exploring all other possible channels.

I looked up a Dutchman who'd worked in Paris for years and asked him for advice. He assured me that the lack of cooperation had nothing to do with my project or with me personally. "Everyone in France avoids taking responsibility; nobody dares to make a decision. First try inviting this administrateur of yours out to lunch. Make sure you choose a good restaurant and a good wine. Talk about his wife and his children, and wait until after coffee before bringing up the real purpose of your visit. Send him a letter, too, with some new information, and say you need a final decision before such-and-such a date. That puts the ball in his court. They're receptive to that sort of thing."

But I couldn't think of anything new to write the administrateur, and a lavish meal with the man was out of the question: I couldn't even reach him over the phone. My only chance was a bureaucratic sneak attack, and that meant that I'd have to find some way of getting my foot in the door of the French government.

That turned out to be easier than I imagined. After a week's worth of phone calls, I got hold of the personal secretary to the Dutch foreign minister. "You mean to say here's an Amsterdammer who wants to go to Amsterdam for a little research and they won't let him?" The man advised me to write a brief report—no more than two sheets of letter paper—and send it to his boss's home address. Would the minister really stand up for me? I could scarcely believe it. But a few days later his secretary assured me that the minister had looked over my report and would try to raise the "Amsterdam issue" with his French colleague during a spare moment at the December European Union summit in Dublin.

Unfortunately for me, however, Franco-Dutch relations were just hitting a record low. It began with a dispute over the consumption of crispy fried migratory birds, a practice in violation of European guidelines. The French prime minister was a great fan of the ortolan, a type of bunting that was caught alive in a net and then killed by piercing its head with a knitting needle. Evidently some people consider its tongue to be a particular delicacy. The Dutch minister tried to ease tensions by noting that bird hunting wasn't high on the European agenda. But just before the meeting in Dublin, French diplomatic sources made it clear that they considered the Dutch to be "Europe's real problem," whereupon the Dutch prime minister called the French president "unstable" and "obsessed" with his war on drugs. Meanwhile, the French ambassador to The Hague avowed that the Dutch tolerance of soft drugs would be the ruin of European youth, and he pointed out that "these Dutch liberties end where French freedom begins." Long before the year was out, I realized that Amsterdam Island had gone unmentioned at the European summit.

THE LOST ISLAND   21

Technically speaking, as the highest-ranking official in the
department, the administrateur had the power to make autonomous
decisions. But he was still subordinate to the Minister of Overseas
Departments and Territories, which is where I decided to focus all
my efforts, ignoring the Department of Southern Lands as much
as possible. My contact at the Dutch Foreign Ministry in The
Hague was hesitant. "You have to make sure that the administrateur doesn't lose face. And going over his head might backfire,
since the superior won't ever step on his toes, at least not publicly.
It will probably only make him dig in deeper. Maybe we should
offer the administrateur a way out by saying that the whole thing
was just a misunderstanding. But I'm not optimistic. The fact that
our ambassador wasn't able to get anywhere should tell you something. He speaks exactly the kind of domineering French they
appreciate, so he even has some clout. Seems like a pretty tough
case, if you ask me."

He was right. When I had been calling the Department of
Southern Lands in the hopes of reaching the administrateur, it
struck me that nearly everyone I spoke to asked the same question:
"On whose behalf are you calling?" I never knew how to respond
until I found out what that question meant, and in France at least
it seemed to translate as: What connections do you have to the
inner circle of my superior? Now that I'd decided to bypass the
administrateur, I needed someone who could introduce me to the
Minister of Overseas Departments and Territories.

The chief secretary of the Dutch Embassy suggested approaching the French writer Jean-Paul Kauffman. The Islamic Jihad had
once held him hostage for more than eleven hundred days in a
darkened cellar in Beirut. After his release, "in order to surround

the ravages that I bore inside me," he had visited the Kerguelen Islands, with the permission of the previous administrateur.

Kauffman had good contacts at the cabinet level and seemed willing to ask the Minister of Overseas Departments and Territories to grant my request. "Amsterdam Island has a fasinating history, especially in relation with its neighbor Saint-Paul. But don't expect too much from my efforts; French bureaucrats seldom reconsider their decisions," he warned me.

He'd spent two days on the island, free to go wherever he liked. He hadn't seen any evidence of secret research or military activities. "But the place is haunted with suicides. People get depressed very quickly out there. That's why Amsterdam always causes more problems for the administration than any other district."

In the middle of February the minister told Kauffman that he had instructed the administrateur "to carefully review the Van Cleef file" and that he would get back in touch with the writer.

It sounded good, and yet I had the feeling that even the minister's evident goodwill would be of little help, since it was still the administrateur who made the final decision, and he seemed like the kind of bureaucrat who stuck to his guns, even with the minister.

I'd done whatever I could, but the more I went at it, the more I seemed to get caught up in an endless chain of contacts with diplomats, politicians, government ministers, and other officials. The project had degenerated into a series of letters written in reference to other letters, into a self-perpetuating cycle of occasionally promising, but never definite, developments.

Once again I began neglecting my friends and retreated to the peace and quiet of various libraries, where I spent months searching for seventeenth-century ships' logs. I shut myself up in a world of misty volcano peaks and brooding albatrosses.

Shortly after New Year's I turned to a sailing magazine for help. I couldn't bear the thought that all my efforts had been in vain; I couldn't allow myself to give up. The only way out seemed to be for me to travel to Amsterdam on my own, with or without permission, and once I was there, refuse to leave. If I planned it right, I could manage a few weeks on the island before the *Marion Dufresne* was scheduled to return. If they wanted to get rid of me before then, they'd have to send a naval ship to remove me.

"You want to sail to Amsterdam? Well, that's a first," said the magazine's acting editor, after locating the island on the map. "I know sailors from all over the world, but I've never heard of anyone going there."

The editor put me in touch with Henk, an ex-sociologist and professional yachtsman. He was a short man, with untamed gray hair and teeth that testified to a wild life. He belonged to a select group of pros who casually talked about "heading down to Rio to pick up a little boat"—a club you couldn't join unless you'd made a couple trips around the world sailing solo. Together we pored over a map of southern Africa. "The best thing would be to rent a yacht somewhere in the general region. You could look for a crew there, too. Going from Australia is out of the question on account of the headwinds—you'll have to sail from west to east. Réunion is a possibility, but there's not much chance of finding a boat there. The best starting point is South Africa, the area around Cape Town, but you might have a hard time finding people adventuresome enough—and that's the kind of people you're going to need. Real sea rovers like that keep their boats moored farther off, in out-of-the-way coves, since they don't have to pay. And that doesn't make them easy to find."

Factoring in wind, current, and distance—at least two thousand miles—Henk estimated that the voyage from South Africa to Amsterdam would take a good three weeks. "And three weeks back, but it would be better just to sail on to Australia. Are you an experienced sailor? No? Do you know what you're getting yourself into? The Indian Ocean's pretty dangerous," he said, rolling himself a cigarette. "Because it's the confluence of a number of marine currents. Warm currents run into cold ones, and that causes tropical depressions and storms, and to top it all off, there's no landmass to hold them back. Down there it's hurricane season practically all year long."

Henk knew a Dutchman who was taking part in a Spanish expedition to retrace Magellan's route around the world. "That might be something for you. They start out in Panama, and from there they sail across the South Pacific. That part of the trip alone takes six months. But I should tell you: I caught a few goofs in their brochure right away. They put the discovery of the Galápagos Islands two centuries before it happened, and that sort of thing makes you wonder how much care was taken with the whole expedition."

Three weeks later, Henk called back. "It's a done deal."

"What do you mean?"

"It's all set. We'll go together. Like I told you, at the moment I'm building a little ship. Small, but seaworthy. Small enough to fit into a container and be transported on a freighter. That's how she'll get to South Africa. We'll take a plane. It's going to be a hell of a trip, one long hard pull, that's for sure. And things'll be pretty cramped, just a hair over twenty-one feet. There are two bunks, but not much else. Think of it as a car on water. We'll be leaving from Durban, at the beginning of next year. I'll be in touch."

I was no sailor and had absolutely no ambition to become one, but I was willing to do anything to reach my goal. I was prepared to raid my savings to finance the trip. I consulted a number of nautical handbooks such as the *South Indian Ocean Pilot*. I agreed with Henk that January was the best month to leave since it would be summertime, and slightly less stormy around Amsterdam than during the rest of the year.

But that didn't apply to the rest of the route. About the waters around South Africa, I read: "The period from December to April seldom goes by without one major storm per month, and in some years there may be two to three tropical storms in the first three months of the year." I also learned that "rough to very rough seas" were a frequent occurrence all year round near Amsterdam Island, as were swells of twenty feet and higher. "Around the fortieth parallel, sailboats have to cut through towering waves that make them reach breakneck speeds."

After three weeks on the open sea, we'd finally catch sight of the peak of Amsterdam, from a distance of sixty miles in clear weather.

Upon approaching the island one must exercise the utmost caution. The coast consists of high, bare and vertical cliffs, which are almost permanently battered by a relentless wash. The prevailing winds are from the west and are generally so strong that there is always a chance of being slammed into the rocks. The coast is very steep and particularly treacherous in fog, because soundings do not give a very good indication of the proximity of land.

Unless the administrateur supérieur decrees otherwise, disembarkations on Amsterdam take place on the pier, a small strip of lava where mooring is very complicated and potentially dangerous. In calm weather it is possible to come ashore by jumping across a few flat rocks, which stick out just above the waterline, offering a modicum of protection. Unloading passengers or cargo is done by means of an onshore crane. As a result of the enormous swells, these operations are generally difficult and sometimes impossible to perform. The anchorages are exclusively temporary. There is no drinking water available. Little food, with the exception of fish. Doctor. Hospital. Marine radio connection.

My folder "Amsterdam by sail" filled up with clippings. I read about passing fronts that show up on the horizon like a ruler; about waves over sixty-five feet high; about the dangers of whales. Which was better after a shipwreck: drinking urine and seawater or slowly dying of thirst? I found myself in a world where ships struck waves with such force, they took on vast amounts of water and crews had to cling to their sails for dear life to keep from being blown into the sea. Anyone who fell overboard was a goner. "Even if the drowning man has a beacon, you're already a couple miles away before you can get your spinnaker down. Then just try to find him when it's dark and the weather's rough."

I also followed the account of a prestigious French round-the-world solo sailing race. Almost two thousand miles southwest of Australia, in the southern part of the Indian Ocean, two of the contestants sent out emergency signals after getting caught in a storm.

"The stretch of ocean in which the sailors capsized is one of the most inhospitable places on earth. Between the fortieth and fiftieth parallels—known as the roaring forties—the wind blows mercilessly around the world from west to east, unchecked by any land." The two missing sailors were eventually rescued. One of them—a fifty-six-year-old Englishman—was trapped for five days in an air pocket underneath his capsized vessel. He lost a piece of his fingertip and was left with a frozen foot. As soon as he'd been hoisted on board the naval frigate that had rescued him, he'd asked for a cup of tea.

A few weeks after my last conversation with Henk, I met someone who knew a little more about him. "Outstanding sailor, no question about it. But he's also a romantic adventurer whose only goal in life is testing his own limits; he always has to push himself just a little further." I again took out my copy of Henk's book *Four Summers at Sea*, which he had inscribed for me with the line "And now onto Amsterdam Island." Under the motto "Setting sail is nothing more than casting off and never docking at the same quay twice," my future sailing partner described an expedition to the Azores, which he had undertaken in a boat the same size as the one we would be taking to Amsterdam. "A boat of no less than twenty feet can be quite seaworthy. In high waves it acts somewhat like a child's tumble toy, easy to knock down but quick to right itself—provided that it's been built to be unsinkable, that is."

When he lay in his bunk at night, during a rainstorm, his cabin felt like a coffin, Henk wrote, because the hatch he had to close was no more than thirty centimeters above his head. I read about his ready-made dinners, about the water that had to be pumped out of the boat every day, about the swelling on his elbow that was oozing pus before he lanced it with a razor-sharp diver's knife.

At the end of February I called him up. "Henk, I don't want to go."

"I figured as much."

"I've got nothing against making the voyage with you as skipper," I went on, "but only on a fairly large yacht, with more people on board than just the two of us. The more comfortable, the better. Besides, I'm not just an *inexperienced* sailor, I'm a complete landlubber. I'm prepared to hang from a rope every now and then, but mainly I just want to gaze at the horizon and let the others do the sailing."

Henk did not seem the least bit impressed by my fear of huge waves, whales, and hurricanes. Nor did he accept the view that a larger ship with more reefable sail was better equipped to weather a storm. But in the end he agreed to leave his own boat in the Netherlands and get in touch with some sailing friends in South Africa who could help us find something bigger.

We spoke again in mid-March. It turned out he'd been a bit too optimistic. He was almost finished working on his boat, but first he had to go to Chile. Then to a maritime expo. And then to Spain. "But don't worry, Alfred, I spoke to Jaap, a Dutchman who lives in Durban. He's willing to charter a big boat for you and sail it to Amsterdam. No problem."

Henk asked me to meet him the following weekend at a yacht club that was located right across from the biggest brothel in Amsterdam. I found him together with Jaap, who was planning to spend the next few months in Europe. There they sat, reclining in the sun, each with a bottle of beer. Both of them were wearing white shorts and slightly soiled shirts.

"I always use a swivel to fish, so the line won't get kinked up," Henk was saying. "And I wrap the line around the winch, so I can hear it if it starts to rattle. Then you go and haul it out. But you need some pretty heavy workman's gloves." They handed me a bottle of beer and, without paying any further attention to me, continued their conversation about chip logs, spray hoods, tapered masts, and backstays.

Jaap looked me over. "There's no reason to worry," he said. "Henk and I once got caught in Hurricane Andrew in a thirty-footer. This is no big deal."

Jaap had studied in Wageningen and worked in "pharmaceutics"—as he put it. He was sixty years old, had three children and a couple grandchildren. He'd lived in Durban most of his life. Once upon a time he'd been married to a South African, but they'd been divorced for twenty years. He'd started sailing five years earlier and immediately took to the open seas, traveling to Polynesia, the Caribbean, West Africa. Henk had trained him, and I had better believe that Jaap was a hell of a sailor himself. Of course he still had nightmares about the time he fell overboard in the Atlantic. He'd survived because he'd tied himself to a lifeline, which he normally didn't do. Then there was the time a mast had fallen and nearly crushed him, but he didn't think too much about that anymore.

The three of us bent over a rather inexact map of the world. Jaap proposed the same southerly route used by the single-handed racers. That way we would avoid the more northerly high-pressure area and keep us out of reach of the hurricanes, which never went south but always struck toward Réunion and Madagascar. We'd have to take a forty-footer at least. Jaap was soon going to America to pick up one just that size and sail it back for its new owner; maybe that would be something for us.

Jaap had never sailed the roaring forties before, but was certain we could manage the seventeen hundred miles from Durban to Amsterdam. "In winter the wind will damn near blow you off your feet, but in the summer things are better. A little variable, but relatively calm. Now and then you'll get a good thirty-knot wind, of course, but there's also a chance of heavy storms. Everything's extreme in the south."

"And what happens if we capsize?" I asked.

"We'll take along an emergency transmitter. The signal gets picked up by a satellite. If you get into trouble, the whole world comes to your rescue."

Henk protested. "If I choose to risk my life by going on a journey like this, I'm not going to burden others with the task of having to fish me out of the water."

"So what's my role?" I asked.

"You'll have to keep watch just like the rest of us. At night that means looking out for any lights that might lead to a collision. And calling the skipper if you see something." We set the fifteenth of November as a provisional departure date. Jaap had a job to do in England and would get in touch with me when he was back in the Netherlands.

Not long after that I heard a crackly message on my answering machine. "Alfred, it's Jaap. I just wanted to, well, we've run into a couple problems and . . . I'll try you again later."

He called back the next day.

"Are you back from England already?" I asked him.

"Yeah, I'm back all right. I got *blown* back. Bloody wind. My sails are shot to hell." He told me he'd just found a great deal on a nice houseboat and was planning to stay in the Netherlands and not return to South Africa. "But don't worry. Our friend Jimmy can do it just as well. The only catch is that I don't have his number, and Henk is on the Wadden Islands at the moment and I can't reach him. But I'm not going to leave you high and dry, because I think it's a great plan. I'll also keep trying to see if my friend Sam can find you a boat to charter." It was our last conversation.

"As you know, the minister has asked the administrateur to reexamine your case," said the spokeswomen for the Ministry of Overseas Departments and Territories at the end of April. "And he has done so."

"That's great. So when can I get started on my project?" I asked.

"I should tell you that the administrateur has already let the minister know that he sees no reason to revoke his earlier decision. That problem is that there are too few people on site to supervise you."

"I'm researching the Dutch history of Amsterdam. All I'm planning to do is look for traces of Willem de Vlamingh, and you want to keep me from doing it?"

"They're not allowed to let you on the island without supervision. At least not during the day." She giggled. "I'm sorry, I was told to take care of the matter, I'm afraid I can't do anything more to help you. There's a budget crunch and a shortage of personnel."

"I don't need any personnel," I said.

"But we do. We have to make sure you're supervised."

I wanted to know what was so risky about my staying on Amsterdam that they needed to keep me under guard, but she said she didn't have any more detailed information.

Jean-Paul Kauffman was willing to approach the Minister of Overseas Departments and Territories one more time, with the message that I was prepared, if necessary, to sign a statement in which I took full responsibility for my own safety on the island.

Meanwhile the French president had called for new elections, and there was a chance that the Minister of Overseas Departments and Territories would not be returning to his post. The same was true for the prime minister, who had already lost his prestige because of some improprieties involving luxury apartments in Paris. Later that month he submitted his resignation after a crushing defeat in the first round of the elections, an act that reminded his greatest political opponent of a "fighter pilot launching his ejector seat four hundred meters before the crash." In May the political crisis became a national calamity when it was announced that the number of French restaurants with a Michelin star had once again fallen. In early June, after the second and final round of elections, victory fires were lit along the boulevard Saint-Germain while drumming demonstrators heaped scorn on the outgoing prime minister's party, to which the Minister for Overseas Departments and Territories also belonged. French progressives celebrated an unprecedented victory, but it seemed likely that Kauffmann's personal letter on my behalf—or, in the worst case, my whole file—would end up with the rest of the departing regime's wastepaper, in accordance with French custom.

In one fell swoop three of my contacts (Jean-Paul Kauffman, the minister's spokesman, and the reputed best friend of the minister's

closest adviser, whom I had also approached) had lost their lines to
the center of power and could no longer help me in any way. Nevertheless I sensed a new opportunity. After all, nothing in France
would be the same: The change of regime also meant a new Minister of Overseas Departments and Territories. And whatever kind
of person he might be, he was bound to be a political opponent of
the current administrateur. I could resume my fight.

I called the personal secretary to the Dutch foreign minister,
explained the situation to him, and asked him if our minister
would still be willing to plead my case. "You can take it from me,"
he assured me, "that he'll send a note to his French colleague in
Overseas Territories."

But when nothing had happened by the end of summer, I decided I
would take the December boat anyway, as the administrateur had
once suggested—i.e., as a regular passenger intending to see the place
for a day or two. Then, upon my arrival in Amsterdam, I would try
to win over the local leaders, and hope they would let me stay. After
all, Amsterdam was a long way from Paris. I again got in touch with
Madame Clément, requesting a reservation—and naturally repeat-
ing my petition to be granted a one-month stay on the island.

In mid-September I received a letter from the administrateur.
"Pursuant to your request," he said he had reserved me a cabin on
the *Marion Dufresne,* which would be departing Réunion for the
Southern Lands on December 1. Whatever else happened, at least
it was now certain that I would be able to set foot on the island,
although my excitement faded as I read on. The ship would be
anchored off the coast of Amsterdam for two days, during which
time I would be allowed to visit the island under supervision—but

only during the day. At night I would have to return to the ship. And even this brief stay could not be guaranteed, since weather conditions could hamper the debarkation, and provisioning was always the top priority.

They had calculated the cost of the trip; I was to transfer the specified amount to the Treasury of the French Republic not later than ten days prior to departure. The letter also contained four forms from the medical branch of the department. Because of the severe natural conditions and absolute isolation, and especially "the extreme distance from full medical facilities," any stay in the Southern Territories demanded "optimal physical condition." I was warned about "intense physical exertion, rough conditions during the passage and disembarkation, low temperatures and very strong winds." Before the head of the medical branch would give his approval, I had to undergo a number of tests, including an electrocardiogram.

But there proved to be other obstacles as well. As the result of an online appeal, I spoke with a Belgian ham radio enthusiast who had spent two weeks with nineteen other men on the Australian Antarctic island of Heard. They had set a new world record for "transmitting and receiving from remote locations": 80,673 radio contacts. "What kind of messages were you sending?" I asked him over the phone, but the content of the transmissions was apparently beside the point. The amateur broadcasters had chartered the *Marion Dufresne* to ship them, together with thirty tons of equipment, to Heard Island via Kerguelen—at a cost of more than two hundred thousand dollars. "There's something funny about all those southern islands," he told me. "They'll let you go, but only as long as they have complete control over everything you do."

One thing the Belgian said stuck with me. He and the other non-French participants had had to apply for a visa for the Southern Lands, in their country of origin. The administrateur had said nothing about that in his letter. I called the French consulate in Amsterdam, where a staff member confirmed the visa requirement. "Your request will then be forwarded to Paris, as the administrateur supérieur is personally responsible for all immigration policy in the Southern Lands."

By neglecting to mention the visa requirement, it seemed that he had played his final trump card: Without a visa, I would be unable to leave the ship and would only be able to look at Amsterdam from the upper deck. It seemed unlikely that this was a simple oversight, since he was the one who issued the visas. For the first time I felt I had concrete evidence that the administrateur was intentionally trying to thwart my plans.

As the day of my departure drew near, it began to dawn on me that I had lost my battle with the Department of Southern Lands. I had booked a plane ticket to Réunion and mailed the results of my medical tests to Paris; Madame Clément had rattled off a number of items, and crossing them off my list one by one, I had bought them all: foul-weather gear, oilskin jacket, boots, and extra-dark sunglasses. I went to the French consulate to pick up my visa and found a whole French class on a field trip admiring the page-long document with its unique stamps. But I despaired at the thought that all these efforts were for just two days on the island where I wasn't even permitted to sleep and where I would be under constant supervision—assuming that the weather was good enough to let me land there at all.

In mid-October, through the Association of the Friends of the Southern and Antarctic Lands, I got in touch with an Amsterdam veteran from Paris. He seemed incredulous. "Just two days? That's nothing. Besides, everyone will be busy with the harbor operation and the mail. There won't be time for outsiders. That's actually the strangest part of your stay on the island: You spend months waiting for the *Marion Dufresne,* and then, when she finally gets there, you can't wait for her to leave. Whenever the boat arrives, it's like a cruel invasion that completely disrupts the isolation."

I told him of my plan to hide if necessary and stay behind on the island. "That won't work," he said. "The boat would never leave without you."

I still had a month to turn up the heat on the French authorities, and as far as I was concerned, the battle still wasn't over. In the middle of October, the mayor of the city of Amsterdam told me he was prepared to ask the French Minister of Overseas Departments and Territories to allow me to stay on the island for a whole month, to uncover traces of Willem de Vlamingh, "particularly in light of the special ties between the two Amsterdams."

Around the same time there was a Summit of Francophone Nations—a loose alliance of French-speaking countries, which collectively seeks to counter Anglo-American dominance in the world. To camouflage the fact that the importance of French outside France was steadily declining, countries like Bulgaria, Nigeria, Moldavia, and Albania were also invited.

Seen in that light, it came as no surprise that Amsterdam Island was included on the "world map of French-speaking territories," which had been published in *Le Monde* especially for the occasion. There was something to this: After all, every one of the island's seventeen residents spoke French; occasionally there were even a couple more. But the fact that the map also listed Saint-Paul— population: zero—did hint at some measure of despair.

In the meantime I managed to reach by phone the "technical adviser for communications" to the new Minister of Overseas Departments and Territories, a prepossessing man with a good sense of humor, who seemed to take a liking to me. While he didn't realize I had led the administrateur to believe I was accepting the offer to spend only two days on the island, he didn't quite see what problem there could be with my staying longer. "There's nothing but brants and penguins out there, right?" The minister was currently dealing with "a number of weighty issues," but the adviser would see what he could do.

Early in November he phoned me up, rousting me from my bed. He sounded keyed up. He had been to a meeting of the highest-ranking officials from all the Overseas Departments and Territories. "During the break I spoke to the administrateur of the Southern Lands about your case. The man was so mad that I'd gotten involved, he started shouting at me. I probably shouldn't be saying this, but in my whole career as a civil servant, I've never seen anyone fly off the handle like that. Whenever I mentioned your name, he would burst into a rage. He referred to a letter he'd sent you, where he presumably laid everything out, and told me that he'd also informed the Dutch ambassador in Paris and the French ambassador to the Netherlands of the reasons for his decision."

"Can't the minister overrule him?"

"The problem is that the minister really can't intervene in a case like this. You see, this isn't some kind of dictatorial hierarchy. The administrateur may be subservient to the ministry, but he does have some margin of autonomy. And I don't think he's about to change his mind."

I was set to fly to Réunion a week later, and now everything seemed lost. Awkwardly I grabbed at my last chance. "I don't suppose you might like to have lunch with me sometime," I said.

"I'm sorry, but I'm booked solid for lunches this month. But if you want, we can meet the day after tomorrow at my office here in Paris."

In the middle of the stairs leading to the métro station I saw a man slumped over, motionless. He was holding an overturned drum, and surrounded by scraps of food. I was among the hundreds of other passengers who went out of their way to avoid him. I was also in a hurry, since there were still seven métro stops, a security gate, and an anteroom with chandeliers between the minister's adviser and me. When I finally stood face-to-face with him, I told him all about the administrateur's failure to inform me of the visa requirement, which I considered a conscious act of deception. "It smacks of sabotage," I said, "since he's the one who has to issue the visa." The adviser nodded. He held up a sheet of paper. "This is the letter our minister received yesterday from the mayor of Amsterdam," he said. "That clearly says something about the level of support you have. It seems to me the only option you have left is to meet the minister in person. Frankly I think this would be justified, given your credentials, and you can count on me to make the arrangements."

"Did you come to Paris just to see me?" Madame Clément asked the next morning in the reception area of the Department of Southern Lands. We hadn't seen each other in twenty months, but we'd spoken on the phone dozens of times since our last meeting. For the most part she'd been aloof and indifferent, although never downright unfriendly. But now that I was officially registered as a passenger on the *Marion Dufresne,* her eyes looked less defensive than the last time I had seen her.

Without waiting for an answer, she took out the documents she had put together for me. "Have you made it to the library of the Polar Institute yet, as I suggested?"

I had decided to say nothing about my conversation at the Ministry of Overseas Departments and Territories and my possible meeting with the minister, so that there'd be no chance of the administrateur's taking possible countermeasures. "No, I haven't had the time," I said, deliberately keeping my answer short.

Without being asked, Madame Clément then informed me that the administrateur had arranged "a special extra-low" fare for me. "You'll see, it will be a lovely trip. As far as Amsterdam itself, I spent two days there myself once, and it may sound strange coming from me, but somehow I got the impression I wasn't very welcome."

As if to drive home her point, she described what she called a "horrible civil war" that had recently occurred not far from Amsterdam. A Taiwanese fishing boat had been two days east of the island when it sent out an SOS. The *Marion Dufresne* happened to be in the area and, responding to the call, found the fishing boat circling around with no fishing lights. The crew members had killed one another off in a knife fight. "The dead Filipinos had been thrown overboard, and the dead Taiwanese were lying in the cold storage among the frozen fish. Things like that happen, you know."

She opened her file folder. "I understand your disappointment," she said gently. "But it's not my decision. Come on, I'll make you a copy of the article about the wreck of the *Princess of Wales.*"

"You can speak to the minister tomorrow," said my contact at Overseas Territories two days later over the phone, after I was already back in Amsterdam. "I squeezed you in between two other appointments. I'll give him a short rundown on your case beforehand. You'll have to be very direct, make sure you don't waste any time. This is your only chance, so don't let it pass you by. I can't make any promises. I have no idea if the minister will be able to do anything for you." He didn't need to tell me it was my last opportunity; I was scheduled leave for Réunion in four days.

The climax of my campaign against the Department of Southern Lands took place in the well-guarded headquarters of Overseas Territories. I sat down in the anteroom, where a display of wall clocks showed what time it was in such pillars of the French empire as Saint-Pierre and Miquelon, French Guiana, and Guadeloupe.

I was well prepared for my conversation with the minister. With a fair degree of precision I was able to reconstruct the course of my protracted conflict with the administrateur and refute all of his declared objections. I knew his weak points. I was aware of his political position and the escalating power struggle between Southern

Lands and the Antarctic Institute, which had been assuming more and more authority and which was at odds with the administrateur over the admittance policy for scientists and the use of the *Marion Dufresne*'s helicopter. All I'd heard about the minister, however, was that he looked "pale as a bidet" and was known to be "frosty and conservative."

I was ushered to a wide hallway with thick shag carpeting, where seven others were already waiting. Every fifteen minutes or so, the wide door to the minister's office swung open, hands were shaken, and words of thanks were uttered. Occasionally an entire delegation would emerge at once. My appointment was scheduled for the end of the afternoon, but it was eight thirty before my name was called. "Everything ran overtime," the technical assistant whispered to me. "You have even less time than I expected."

I shook the minister's hand and began to plead my case. I knew that when it came to Amsterdam, I had a tendency to regale any possible listener with the history of the island from the Pleistocene epoch on, but I managed to control myself and focus on the subject of Willem de Vlamingh.

"That sounds like a fine plan to me," said the minister. "I'd like to visit Amsterdam myself one day. When does your flight leave?"

"There's no airport," said his assistant. "You can only get there by boat. Monsieur Van Cleef is booked as a passenger for the voyage in December. The *Marion Dufresne* returns to Amsterdam in January, so he would be able to spend exactly one month on the island."

"I see nothing wrong with that," said the minister. "I suggest you approach the administrateur and put the matter before him." I held my breath. The technical assistant leaned over to the minister and said something I couldn't understand. "Right," said the minister. "Then from this moment on, your sojourn on Amsterdam is a ministerial decree." He stood up and shook my hand. "I will have the director of my cabinet write a letter to the administrateur, ordering him to see to the details of your journey, in view of its importance for Franco-Dutch relations."

"You're my hero," I said as I took my leave of the adviser.

Flushed with victory I called the administration of the Southern Lands. "On whose behalf are you calling?" asked the phone receptionist. "On behalf of the minister." I was transferred to Madame Clément. She did not congratulate me; in fact, she didn't even mention my meeting with the minister. She sounded the same as always.

"You're leaving in a few days, correct? So you'll be on board with the administrateur. He's taking his official tour at the same time."

"What a coincidence," I said, as neutrally as possible. "Could you tell me when the January boat will be coming to pick me up?"

"There is no January boat this year," she said. "You should have left earlier. The next sailing will be in February, and the one after that, four months later. I would suggest you try again next year."

I felt everything crumble away underneath me. I wanted to curse at her, but I couldn't.

"Well, then, I guess it will be a three-month trip. I'll come back on the February boat," was all I said.

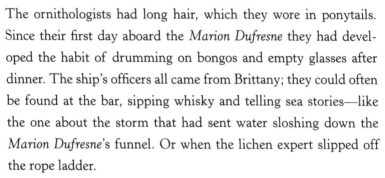

The ornithologists had long hair, which they wore in ponytails. Since their first day aboard the *Marion Dufresne* they had developed the habit of drumming on bongos and empty glasses after dinner. The ship's officers all came from Brittany; they could often be found at the bar, sipping whisky and telling sea stories—like the one about the storm that had sent water sloshing down the *Marion Dufresne*'s funnel. Or when the lichen expert slipped off the rope ladder.

One of the officers entertained me with tales of the glory days, when the Compagnie Générale Maritime still had a fleet of more than a hundred ships, and when you could get fresh baguettes in the farthest reaches of Southeast Asia and Africa—concrete proof that France had been an empire. But what he remembered most of all was the abundance of time. Sometimes they would stay in port for two weeks. "But these days all you have is half a day to enjoy yourself, so it doesn't make much difference whether it's penguins you're after or nightlife."

The largest group of passengers consisted of scientists and recent post-docs doing research in one of the Southern Lands as part of their national service. Then there were the technicians who'd been contracted to do maintenance work—carpenters and plumbers with beards and checkered shirts.

All these passengers stuck together in groups, which led to all kinds of secret meetings, arguments, and other incidents that I either missed completely or only learned about later: the party the volcanologists had staged on the upper deck; the ship's female doctor sneaking nightly into the cabin of the meteorologist; the sighting of three whales. More than ever I had the feeling I didn't belong.

During the first few days at sea, when the temperature was still bearable, I would lean over the railing for hours. While I was there I struck up a conversation with a man of about forty, an antiques dealer who had paid a fortune to take the cruise Réunion-Crozet-Kerguelen-Amsterdam-Réunion. "You know, every work of art has a space around it," he said. "I've sold that emptiness for years. Now I'm living off my investments." Then we stared a long time at the flying fish leaping through the spray, without saying another word.

The humidity slowly dissipated. We left the regular sea-lanes and moved into a stretch of ocean completely devoid of other ships, following a southwestern course set for total emptiness. As if to celebrate our collective isolation, on the fourth day the captain invited everyone to a lavish open-air buffet on the helicopter landing deck. Passengers and crew filled their plates with fresh lobster and salad, and quenched their thirst with wine or *planteur maison*, the house variety of planter's punch. The Malagasy day laborers helped the waiters turn the lambs on the spit, and the captain treated all the guests to an aperitif.

Above the tables with champagne and white wine was an enormous French flag, which spanned the entire breadth of the ship. Underneath it were a number of smaller flags: the flag of the Antarctic Institute, the Breton flag, and—in honor of the seismologists from the earthquake institute in Tokyo—the Japanese flag. Naturally the flag of the Southern Lands had also been hung up, displaying the regional coat of arms: two sea elephants supporting a shield crowned by a coronet adorned with two anchors. The shield itself was quartered into sections of azure and or, which depicted a royal penguin for Crozet Island, a silver Kerguelen cabbage, a silver iceberg for Terre Adélie, and a black lobster for Amsterdam and Saint-Paul. There was no Dutch flag.

The official portion of the event consisted of a welcome speech by the captain, followed by a full-throated anthem sung to the tune of "God Save the Queen," which, loosely translated from the French, would sound something like:

Grandfather's testicles
Hang from the ceiling now
Shrunken and dried
Grandmother's in despair
Cries when she see them there
She'd never known a better pair
Anywhere in town.

The administrateur hadn't left his cabin for days; rumor had it he was too seasick to stand. Now he was sitting at one of the long tables, between the first mate and the wife of the helicopter pilot; I was diagonally across. He was wearing checkered pants and a blue button-down shirt, holding an extended monologue on marine plankton; he tended to spit whenever he talked. Every so often one of his tablemates would try to interject something, only to be ruthlessly cut off. I was reminded of our one previous conversation over the phone, when he had done exactly the same thing.

The man evidently enjoyed tossing out percentages and statistics. He knew exactly how many pygmy right whales were in which ocean and how many tons of illicitly caught Chilean sea bass Japan imported annually. I wanted to ask him why he'd tried to thwart my plans and why he'd ignored me for the past couple years and what it was like for him to have to take his official tour with me of all people, but I said nothing. Finally I blurted out over the blueberry *bavaroise*, "Could you explain why I need a visa for my visit to Amsterdam?"

For a moment the administrateur fixed me with a cold, vacant stare. He demonstratively turned to the first mate and began telling him how he had been recently refused entry to South Africa, quite by mistake, because they thought his visa had expired. After he had finished, I said, "You still owe me an answer to my question."

The administrateur first told another anecdote, about a Frenchman who had fallen afoul of Australia's immigration policy, but eventually he interrupted himself. "I know nothing about the visa policy for the Southern Lands," he lied. "That's the responsibility of the French Embassy. When we reach Amsterdam, the district chief will verify your identity. He'll decide whether you are to be allowed onto the island. Now, if you'll excuse me, I'm expected elsewhere."

He stood up and walked over to the bar, where he poured a cup of coffee from one of the thermoses. He lit a cigar and continued his conversation with the wife of the helicopter pilot.

Now that I was really on my way to the remotest island on earth, I felt a growing emptiness, as if I were sucking up the space around me. I wasn't depressed, I wasn't happy, I wasn't excited: I felt nothing.

I continued to collect random bits of information. On the bridge I asked the captain about the ship's displacement, draft, and maximum speed; about the number of cabins and cranes on board; the length of the container deck, types of diesel motors, the worst storm he'd ever experienced—taking it all down on one of my many notepads. I quizzed the scientists about their work, what they found so fascinating about cones, craters, lava flows, earthquakes, flies, weaver birds, painted lady butterflies, killer whales, white-bellied storm petrels, lichens, and radon levels.

There was also a professor on board who did research on scientists in remote areas. Although I'd never heard of him, he was apparently famous all over the world, or at least back en métropole. He was studying how well humans adapt to extremely hostile environments, prolonged isolation, and a diet of canned food.

But the most intriguing conversations were with a Flemish specialist in rotifers, named Willem De Smet. He was on his way to the Crozet Islands. "A golden opportunity—I'll probably discover some new species. We don't know a thing about Crozet."

De Smet was a veteran in exploring the ends of the earth. He had spent long periods in isolation in the Arctic: on Bear Island, on Edgeøya (Edge Island). With miniature flasks and plankton nets he was always on the lookout for the microscopic, wormlike rotifers. "At first glance it's not exactly clear how my findings actually benefit people," he said, without a trace of remorse.

Most of the time he could be found by the railing, wearing his sandals—even though it was starting to get colder. "I get claustrophobic in the dining hall or the bar. Far too much smoke. I can't read or write in there. I need the serenity of the water." On Crozet he was planning to join his colleagues who were studying diatoms, which he described as "one-celled plants closed off by lids, like little boxes of Camembert. They keep well, too. Marvelous creatures."

There were vegetarian rotifers, rotifers that ate other rotifers, and rotifers that lived as parasites in the intestinal linings of earthworms. You could find rotifers in the water. In mosses. Between grains of sand. No, there wasn't a De Smet worm yet. But the idea of naming a rotifer after a man was appalling: The male rotifers were complete duds. "Ugly as sin. They don't eat. They don't even have a digestive tract. They just do their reproductive work and die."

Things had reached the point where the overwhelming majority of females reproduced by means of unfertilized eggs. And since they didn't need the males, they'd stopped producing them. In 95 percent of the species, all you can find are females, said the Flemish biologist. The female rotifers had definitively disproved the myth of the male as fertilizer and preserver of the species. Consigned to the compost heap of evolution, the males were becoming increasingly smaller, and their lifespan correspondingly shorter.

The crew kept a chart in a corridor on the lower deck, where they would post the current air and sea temperatures, wind velocity, and the speed of the ship—as well as the number of nautical miles we had traveled and the distance remaining to our first destination, the Crozet Archipelago. But the Southern Lands were so far away from Réunion and so far away from one another and so far away from anything and everything that the end of the first stage never seemed to get any closer.

The swells increased, and the winds grew fiercer. The sky was a dull gray, streaked with dirty black. I saw my first albatross. We had reached "the roaring forties," the endless expanse where the three oceans merge into a single devilish sea that spins around the globe like a furious top that has flung off practically every bit of land. We had sailed "beyond the stars and the sun," as the Greeks would say, to the unbounded regions cruelly ruled by "gloomy darkness and everlasting night." Amsterdam Island lay at 37 degrees southern latitude; before I reached it I had several thousand nautical miles to go, along the edge of the world.

The *Marion Dufresne* had been especially built to service the Southern Lands, and was only a few years old. The ship was named after a eighteenth-century slave trader and explorer Marc-Joseph Marion-Dufresne. One of his missions had been to repatriate the Tahitian chief Ahu-toru, who had been brought to the French court as a living "noble savage." But the Polynesian never made it back, having contracted smallpox on Madagascar. Meanwhile Marion-Dufresne had another, more important assignment, to accomplish what no one before him had been able to do: He would discover the Terra Australis. At the same time, he was commissioned as a privateer to steal a shipload of cinnamon and nutmeg from the Dutch on the Spice Islands.

His two flute-ships followed a southerly course, farther and farther into the unknown. He pressed on despite heavy seas and snowstorms, driven by the hope of eternal glory. For weeks on end he saw nothing but open ocean, until some flying seagulls indicated land was nearby. The next day, during a momentary break in the clouds, the watch discerned the hazy yet unmistakable outline of a cape, which the ships seemed to have narrowly missed. Marion-Dufresne did not have to think long to come up with a name for the new discovery: the Land of Hope.

The following day the slave trader and his men tried to become the first people ever to set foot on the Terra Australis, but the dense fog and overwhelming wind caused their two ships to collide before the men could land, causing heavy damage and the loss of a bowsprit and foremast.

Marion-Dufresne was forced to sail on toward the southeast, past the forty-seventh parallel, where the westerly winds howled. He knew he had to find a harbor somewhere, even if that meant traveling thousands of nautical miles, so that he could repair his ships. At last, land was sighted, and he decided to put in along a coastline that had been designated on nautical charts by Abel Tasman and other Dutch seafarers as Moordenaarsbaai, Murderers' Bay.

They dropped anchor off Waewaetorea Island, northwest of Urupukapuka. They made three camps. The surgeons cared for the sick while the carpenters carved new masts. At first, Marion-Dufresne and his officers crossed themselves a few extra times whenever they headed inland, but soon the sailors developed an unusually amicable relationship with the island's inhabitants. During a ritual gathering, the captain was even presented with four white feathers, a gift reserved for chiefs.

Four days later, however, everything changed. The sailors had cut down a sacred tree, which was taboo even to touch. Marion-Dufresne and twenty-eight of his men were stabbed to death, disemboweled, hacked to pieces, and then eaten. Cooked skulls and half-eaten pieces of human flesh bore silent testimony to the failed expedition along the forty-seventh parallel.

But two discoveries had been made, including an archipelago that would eventually bear the name of Marion's assistant Julien Crozet, and the "Land of Hope," an uninhabitable, gloomy island that would lead a lonely existence under the name Marion. Of course this turned out not to be the edge of the long-sought-after Terra Australis but the peak of a volcanic island, which is almost always hidden from sight, battered black and blue by the fierce west winds. After various twists of fate this pointless bit of land would eventually become a possession of South Africa. Apart from that, the only thing to bear the hapless captain's name is an enormous underwater continental plate.

In the corridor next to the dining hall was an old drawing of two half-naked natives, each holding a pointed stick. The picture bore the caption "The 'noble savage'—the myth believed by Marion-Dufresne."

After nearly a week at sea, a mossy but almost colorless patch of land emerged from the fog like a gray-green ice cube in a glass of splashing water: the Crozet Archipelago. It was raining. It was always raining on Crozet, unless of course it was snowing or hailing.

The harbor was situated on Possession Island, where we spent the next day and a half. The *Marion Dufresne* anchored off a small lava beach, where we were met by five men, two tractors, and a hundred and twenty thousand king penguins: screeching, vomiting, walking up to the water and back, parading, feeding, standing stock still, or even dying. Some twenty people stayed on the island—scientists, conscripts, and handymen—and an equal number boarded the ship. They were headed back to Réunion and France, still separated from their loved ones by many weeks at sea. The French flag on the island did not wave; it was made of iron.

"I spent a year and a half on Crozet working as a cook," said the man who sat down next to me at the bar the afternoon the *Marion Dufresne* again raised anchor. "Somebody once tried to chop off my head with a kitchen knife. He'd gone crazy—partly from the lack of women, but what really pushed him over the edge was the absence of trees. Some people just can't deal with that." The cook himself had fallen into a deep depression when he went back to France. "I didn't want to go out for weeks." He took a swig of his planteur maison. He told me how he couldn't fit in at home anymore, that his life was here, in the Southern Lands. So he'd signed on for a second stint, this time for a year on Kerguelen.

The ship's café was called the Forum. It was separated from the dining hall by frosted-glass walls decorated with penguins and big waves, and had an elliptical bar furnished with lots of steel. The walls and tables were yellow ocher; the blue-green block chairs had loose cushions that slowly gave way when you sat on them. In high swells the chairs would slide back and forth across the dining hall.

After Crozet the only thing you could see abovedecks was spray. For three days we sailed through a tunnel of mist and fog, until after a total of 756 nautical miles we reached Port-aux-Français, which is the capital of all the Southern Lands as well the Kerguelen district. Half-frozen, I wandered among the jumble of barracks. There was only one road—five hundred yards long—and it had a single sign: CAUTION: SEA ELEPHANTS! The capital was obscured by a forest of antennas; its geographic center, the place Charles de Gaulle, was a functionless concrete platform built on the rough, wind-ravaged ground. Bits of wood and plastic swirled through the streets, while a menhir brought from Brittany graced the entrance to the chapel of Our Lady of the Wind.

The next day we left the harbor, sailed passed the Bay of the Southern Dawn, and continued around Kerguelen Island, which is as large as Corsica and surrounded by dozens of smaller islands. The ship moored at a different place every day: There was an abundance of sheltered bays and coves. Occasionally we were allowed to board a small dinghy and go ashore for a few hours.

It was on Kerguelen that the most powerful gust in the history of meteorology had been recorded; the whole place looked as if it had been sanded clean. We glided past lakes, rivers, and gray, weather-beaten hills. Near Sugarloaf Mountain the clouds opened up and we could see the peaks of the glaciers, standing out against the cloudless sky like polished silver knives. We passed tiny Australia Island and the Bay of Disappointment. I saw untouched volcano peaks and half-frozen waterfalls. This was the end of the world: raw, merciless, untouched.

We spent a week in the archipelago, and then the last bit of land—the Cloudy Islands—disappeared over the horizon as we steered north-northeast into the emptiness of the Indian Ocean. In less than three days we would reach Saint-Paul, where we would put in briefly before sailing on to Amsterdam.

We had arrived in the waters where for centuries French sailors had feared the hand of Satan would grab hold of their ship and drag them into the unfathomable abyss. This was where the captain of the *Flying Dutchman* had invoked the devil after storms had kept him from rounding the cape, so that his ship was damned to sail those stormy latitudes until the end of time, a ghost vessel at full sail slicing through whatever ship crossed her path. Any sailor who saw her could only pray to God to change her course.

Those of us planning to stay on Amsterdam began spending more and more time together. I got to know the cook, the butcher, the team of glaziers, the screen repairman (who called himself a mosquiteer), three meteorologists, and two specialists in aerometrics. I felt the strongest bond with Louis, a dreamy ornithologist, still very much a youth, with a searching spirit I found familiar. Louis was longing for the silence of his upcoming stay in the ornithologists' cabin on the most remote part of the island. Every day he could be found on deck, staring at the birds until he got so numb with cold, he had to go in. With great patience he taught me how to distinguish the various species of albatross that flew with the ship.

Although I'd been on board for almost three weeks, I still got lost in the maze of corridors belowdecks, so that I was never sure I'd wind up on Deck B3 or the lower level of Exit A. But I was hardly in a position to complain, since I belonged to the select group of passengers with their own stateroom—containing a shower, a desk, and a framed poster—in my case, Raoul Dufy's *Promenade à Nice*. I had gotten used to the daily rhythm, the four-course meals, the monotony, the waves beating against the ship. Now nothing but water separated me from the island of my desire; I had never been this far away from land.

I was able to look out of my cabin porthole for longer and longer periods without getting queasy, watching the constant play of water and horizon, water and horizon. But the second night after we left Kerguelen I was woken by the heavy storm the captain had announced earlier that day. I turned on the light and saw my bags sliding into the desk chair, where I had draped some clothes. The whole mess went skidding from the one wall to the other at incredible speed. In the hallway I heard other objects rolling back and forth and doors slamming. The ship itself seemed to be creaking everywhere, riddling noises in a world that would never be my own.

The next morning the water sloshed over the high lip of the shower pan, getting some of my luggage wet. I felt nauseated and exhausted. Clutching the steel railings, I pulled myself upstairs and staggered into the dining hall. It was already nearly lunchtime: I had missed breakfast yet again. There were nonslip place mats on the tables. Walls of water and spray heaved against the ship, which groaned under the onslaught as the waiters served *Côte d'agneau et ses légumes*. That day we drank Château de Coulaine Cuvée Diablesse; the tablecloths got soaked with dark red stains. Still holding his glass of wine, one of the Japanese seismologists fell over in his chair, toppling his entire row of fellow diners like dominoes. The second time it happened, the waiters lashed the chairs together.

. . .

By the next morning the storm had died down. The sky was a bright blue, and the air was humid. We were moving farther and farther away from the Antarctic air masses.

"Are you trying to escape something by coming here to the middle of nowhere?" Louis the ornithologist asked me on the upper deck. I told him I was mostly drawn to the place by my longing for the past, for the age of Willem de Vlamingh, for what once had been, but is no longer. He said he understood what I meant, and the two of us went back to gazing at the endlessness around us.

Louis had taken off his Windbreaker to let the summer sun caress his body. He was wearing a T-shirt with penguins; his arms were white and hairless. He was the first one to spot the change of color on the horizon: land.

The ship sailed right up to the crater of Saint-Paul, which was enclosed by steep walls and filled with seawater. The total surface area of the island was less than three square miles. Two sailors went ashore in a little dinghy to pick up the rat and rabbit exterminator, who, along with an assistant and a dog, had spent a month on the uninhabited island. "That's the new district chief," said one of the glaziers. "He'll be our leader on Amsterdam."

The crew took whoever wanted to see the island ashore in a dinghy. Once on land, I climbed the face of the cliff, pulling myself up by the reeds. From above, the collapsed crater, or caldera, of Saint-Paul looked frozen in the void, like an amphitheater after an enormous tidal wave had swept performers and spectators alike into the depths of the sea.

. . .

The *Marion Dufresne* raised anchor at dawn the next morning, and we set off on the last leg of the voyage. As we sailed through a curtain of rain, the sun disappeared; the waves were long and high, the horizon invisible.

The *administrateur* and I had avoided each other the entire journey. I couldn't say for sure whether he would again attempt to torpedo my stay on Amsterdam, but I had felt more optimistic about my chances after seeing The List.

The List was posted outside one of the ship's offices—in this case, that of the chief of provisions and harbor operations. To the left were the names of those passengers restricted to a two nights' stay on Amsterdam; on the right were the men who would be staying behind. I found my name at the very bottom: Vancleef, Alfred: researcher. By order of: XX. Barracks: Sheathbill 7. I had been classified and equipped with an address. Evidently I existed on Amsterdam Island.

I had a glass of whisky at the bar. I was tense and would have gladly put off the actual sighting for just a little longer.

The mist grew progressively denser. We had stowed our baggage in large wooden crates that were to be hoisted ashore. Everyone was standing on the foredeck. A black smudge appeared in the gray curtain of rain and slowly grew into a wall of rock that rose straight out of the water. A dark peak came into view, just barely; it was surrounded by wisps of fog. "The False Peak," said the district chief. We were now so close to Amsterdam, I could hear the barking of fur seals and the faint sound of surf crashing on rocks.

Everything was gray; it was like watching a black-and-white movie on a channel with poor reception.

Graceful albatrosses, seagulls, and petrels glided alongside as we sailed up the island's ragged eastern coast on our way to the landing. This part of the island was undeveloped, untouched. It looked as desolate as it must have appeared in the spyglasses of the old explorers, and exactly as it did in the seventeenth-century sketches I had studied.

Suddenly I saw the first evidence of human presence: the aerometric mast that was pictured on the only stamp that had ever been dedicated to Amsterdam. A little while later, with the help of a pair of binoculars, I was able to make out the concrete pier, a tractor, a group of weather-beaten trees, and, higher up, eight barracks in pastel colors. This was Martin-de-Viviès, the "capital."

"The first time I came here I was shocked at how tiny the island really is," said the district chief. "There have been cases of a men signing on to work here for a year and a half and then refusing to leave the *Marion Dufresne* at the sight of those barracks. They'd rather break their contracts than spend that long on Amsterdam."

The ship dropped anchor. I saw waves battering the cliffs and seals sliding off the pier into the sea. The plan was for us to disembark by jumping into an inflatable rubber boat from a rope ladder dangling by the hull of the ship. We waited for an hour, but nothing happened.

"I'm not exactly optimistic," said the district chief. "With these waves there's a real danger in trying to bring the passengers ashore in the dinghy. That's not uncommon; sometimes the storms are so bad, the helicopter can't land. It's even happened that the captain has decided to turn around and sail the *Marion Dufresne* right back to Réunion, despite the fact it could have been four months since she was last there."

I walked away from the others. In the distance, on the coast, I saw orange raincoats milling about. The rain pelted my face. There was the wayward island of Amsterdam, and it would not be much longer before my conception of the place would have to confront its reality. The *Marion Dufresne* would sail away, and I would never see the administrateur again. I shuddered.

In the meantime they'd already declared that rubber boats were out of the question, given the weather, and since it wasn't likely to clear up anytime soon, they decided to drop us off in the helicopter. The chief of provisions and harbor operations lost no time in drawing up a departure plan.

We assembled by the helicopter platform. First in line was the administrateur, along with the mailbags. Apparently he'd seen too many war films with helicopter rescues, because even though the pilot's wife had told everyone that the most important thing was to stay calm and approach the machine with your head up, he ducked and sprinted as fast as his inflatable life jacket would allow.

Along with the aerometrics specialists and a handyman, I was the last of the passengers to leave the ship. Once we were airborne, we could see how rough and empty the island really was. My hands were sweating: Just thirty seconds separated me from my first step on the island.

We landed before I knew it. I immediately walked to the sign that read BIENVENUE À AMSTERDAM and had one of the glaziers take a picture of me holding my arms to the heavens: After all, my arrival had to be immortalized. The helicopter made two more trips before returning to the ship for good. It was pouring rain, and I was quickly soaked since I'd left my raincoat with my other luggage.

The meteorologists were welcomed by their colleagues already on the island. Louis was met by another ornithologist who would be showing him the ropes. The aerometrics men met their colleagues, glaziers went with glaziers, the new cook with the old one, the new district chief with his predecessor. I looked at the ship in the distance. The dominant sound was the barking of fur seals. I suddenly felt an enormous craving for chocolate.

Alone, I walked down the muddy path, turning right at a signpost that read PARIS 7,316 MILES. I crossed the boulevard Martin-de-Viviès, a small macadam road with barracks on either side. Nearly thirty men had been flown ashore, but there was no trace of any of them; the capital of Amsterdam looked deserted. I stopped at one of the barracks facing the ocean and went inside. Louis was talking to his new colleague. I asked for directions: "The Sheathbill? That's way at the back, between the Penguin and the store," said the ornithologist.

I found my barracks a little ways off, exactly where he said. Room 7 was empty except for a bunk bed with visibly unwashed sheets, a wardrobe with two hangers, and a chair. The cracked window looked out over a little shed, gas canisters, pallets, and crates marked Amsterdam or Southern Lands. From a bag lying on the floor, I surmised that would be sharing my room—I hoped just for as long as the *Marion Dufresne* was at anchor.

I wanted to take a shower, but I hadn't thought to bring a towel. Suddenly I heard a loud, dull banging noise, which first sounded like a couple making love on a squeaky bed. But then I realized it was too regular, too mechanical for that. So I walked down the hall and then outside, in an attempt to track down the source. It turned out that my room was next door to the post office, where there was a yellow mailbox with a timetable indicating that the next collection would be the following evening. Inside, three men were furiously stamping envelopes. "When the ship's at anchor, I'm open twenty-four hours a day," said the postmaster. "Everybody wants to send their letters at the last minute. Don't worry, you won't have to put up with the noise once the ship leaves. I'm closed for the rest of the year."

I asked where I could find a towel. "There aren't any towels on Amsterdam," said one of the men. "You might be able to buy one of those red ones with the emblem of the Southern Lands, but I don't know if they're still in stock."

"When does the store open?" I asked.

"It's closed daily, except on Friday between five thirty and six thirty. So you'll have to drop by in five days."

Still drenched, I wandered through the settlement. I longed for a desk or a writing table, for warm clothes, a book, and—more than anything—a room with a view of the sea. As the last women I would see for months to come, I fixed the faces of the ship's doctor and pilot's wife in my mind as they walked past, my eyes scanning their bodies. At the pier I saw the Malagasies straining as they lugged the wooden crates through the colony of howling fur seals.

At last my bags arrived; I brought them to the Sheathbill in a wheelbarrow. My things were soaked. I washed myself in the sink and dried myself off with a sweater. A big welcome dinner was scheduled for that evening. I put on a clean shirt and my wrinkled suit jacket. I plopped down on my bed. Back home at a moment like this I would have lit up a joint to disperse my gloomy thoughts and soften the sharp edges of my perception.

Only now did I realize the extent to which my image of the island had been formed by all the historical accounts I had read: If a Dutch East India captain dressed in seventeenth-century attire had come walking by I wouldn't have been the least bit surprised. But in reality, Amsterdam was a French island through and through, a fact I simply had to accept. Still, I was annoyed by the French flag fluttering over the boulevard, and by the fact that every letter was stamped with the postmark Martin de Viviès—the leader of the first French mission on the island. The signpost showed the distance to various cities on various continents, but one was conspicuously absent—my own Dutch Amsterdam. And why had I been tucked away in what must have been the most dismal room on the whole island? Could the administrateur of the Southern Lands be responsible for this as well? Was all of this his doing? A kind of petty revenge?

I felt as though I'd driven into some forlorn desert town in the middle of the night, where, having managed to locate a dingy hotel, I plopped down on a spongy mattress, with the thought that, come morning, I'd find some other hotel. Or, failing that, I would leave the town for good. But here, there was no other hotel and no other town. I was stuck on Amsterdam Island. And I had only myself to blame. Of course, the *Marion Dufresne* still lay at anchor, so I had a day and a half left to reconsider. But if I did leave, I would miss out forever on the chance to hear the ship's horn sailing away while I stayed behind on this lost island that had strayed to the edge of the world.

. . .

That evening it was still damp. We walked in groups to a cave just outside the capital. The tables had been set with festive displays of lobster, salads, cheeses, and sauces. Large cuts of fresh beef were roasting on the spit. In honor of the administrateur's visit, the best wines had been brought out, even a few bottles of champagne. The district chief welcomed everyone and then gave the floor to the administrateur.

"Residents of Amsterdam, new and old islanders alike. The variety here in the Southern Lands is astounding! Yesterday the sky was clear blue and we were blinded by the sun in all her beauty; today we arrived in a constant downpour, amid storm and fog. As in the other districts, I am pleased to see how many improvements have been made here, most significantly the preparations for the window replacements and the restructuring of the duty roster. And I have nothing but praise for the outgoing district chief. It is to his credit that this community of civilians and soldiers, scientists and technicians, young people and veterans proudly and energetically perform their daily activities and tasks, driven by one common goal: enhancing our prestige in the Southern Lands and in the world at large."

He carefully folded his paper and slipped it in his inside pocket. "Finally I would like to mention that Monsieur Van Cleef of the Netherlands will be spending a few days here, at the special invitation of the minister and the administration of the Southern Lands. I ask that all of you be of service to him in his interesting research."

Those present applauded. By suggesting I would be staying "a

few days" instead of spending nearly a whole summer, the administrateur was evidently making a final attempt to confuse me, but
he could no longer hold me back. The *Marion Dufresne* would def-
initely be leaving without me.

I could not escape thanking him for his kind words, and joined
the small circle of men around him. He had just begun a lengthy
anecdote about his visit to the Antarctic District, which had been
claimed by its discoverer in 1840 with these words: "My valiant
comrades! Long live the King and long live France! No other
explorer will outshine us here. France reigns supreme on the South
Pole. This vast, uninhabitable land will bear a French name, a name
dearer to me than all others, that of my wonderful companion
through life. Gentlemen, say hello to Adélie! Long live my wife!"

The administrateur was describing how bitterly cold it had
been in Terre Adélie. "Despite this, I decided to go for a five-mile
walk. They had sent a helicopter to pick me up, but after all, a
man has his pride. Anyway, as I was hiking back I turned around
and saw a strong young man who kept jogging up the path and
whizzed right past me. Later I learned he had set a new record for
that particular course. So that evening I posted my own time on
the bulletin board in the dining hall. You know what I wrote
above that?"

When the aerometrics specialist to whom this question was
addressed failed to answer, the district chief decided to save the
situation. Casting a quick glance at the dish with lobster, he asked,
"What?"

"Senior champion."

I shook the administrateur's hand. "You should try the cod,"
he said.

. . .

The next day I went to the "Great Skua" barracks, which housed the dining hall, but when I arrived, there was nothing left. "You're too late for breakfast," said the doctor, a chain-smoker aptly and matter-of-factly known as the Chimney.

I followed the boulevard toward the harbor pier, the only place on the island where a ship could possibly land. The sickly smell of fur seals was everywhere. "It's even worse when the sun comes out," one of the meteorologists had warned me. "But you'll get used to it after a while." A small road with hairpin switchbacks led down to the landing: a narrow, concrete-covered tongue of lava rock that jutted eleven yards into the churning sea. The "harbor" was a dreary sight: two small, corroded hangars, and a few diesel tanks for the power station. Some past resident had planted a cactus, which was still hanging on since the temperature on the island never went below freezing, and since it had somehow managed to survive all the storms. Every few minutes a surge would crash over the pier and dozens of fur seals would be buried in a wall of water.

The provisioning was well underway. Three Malagasy sailors jumped off a rope ladder onto a World War II–period inflatable raft as it was launched from the *Marion Dufresne*. The boat was full of wooden supply crates, fuel barrels, and the remaining luggage—all packed in large nets—and was towed ashore by a dinghy.

The dinghy headed toward the pier. The sea was relatively calm but grew choppier closer to the island. The sailors tossed a line ashore that was caught and tied off on a tractor, then they quickly flattened out on the dinghy, out of the way of the towline. The tractor backed up a ways while the dinghy tugged in the opposite direction; as soon as the raft was more or less in balance, the Malagasies reappeared. It was a risky operation. Almost every year at least one of them got injured trying to land in the ferocious surf.

Using a tall, three-legged derrick crane that was at least forty years old, men in foul-weather gear hoisted the nets off the raft. Every attempt to modernize this operation had ended in failure. None of the new, specially designed boats had survived the landings on Amsterdam, and every addition to the lava tongue had been destroyed by heavy storms and swept into the swirling sea.

"Last time the *Marion* was here," said the Chimney, back in the Great Skua, "they ran into some pretty bad weather. So the provisioning had to be done in a hurry. Later we discovered that instead of the chicken feed we'd ordered, they gave us a triple supply of dishwashing detergent—enough to last for years. So the chickens died, and we went for four months without any eggs or cake."

Just before the *Marion Dufresne* left, I met the departing district chief in the dining hall. He had clear blue eyes, a goatee, and long hair. He was a doctor, a professional soldier, and, by his own admission, a dreamer.

"There's no such thing as isolation," he said. "Even on Amsterdam we're like cogs in a great machine. No matter how secluded we may be, we never stop getting signals from the outside that remind us who we really are."

I had heard that the outgoing chief's leadership style was fairly authoritarian, and that he had banned excursions and meals in small groups. When I asked him about the latter, he said, "That's true. Amsterdam attracts loners who tend to chafe at too many rules. Sometimes they're drifters who are running away from life.

That's why I made sure everyone ate together, every day. That's also the reason I gave them so many jobs—preferably things that had nothing to do with their function on the island. Then they do it as a matter of principle, for the ideal of the community. No one is useless on Amsterdam."

"Would you say that you see the people here as a group of castaways?" I asked.

"Castaways lose their ship, their plans, their future. We, on the other hand, have all gained something. The tragic thing is that we never appreciate something that's alive until it's on the point of dying. All of us leaving today have a strong sense of belonging to a group, but as soon as we're back in the world we left a year and a half ago, that feeling of community will dissolve into nothing."

Amsterdam was a solitary place and had hardly ever been inhabited. Ever since its earliest encounters with the outside world, the island appeared to have learned to defend itself. From the first human sighting, the island had shrouded itself in heavy weather. As soon as the island sensed the *Marion Dufresne* approaching, the barometric pressure would drop and it would invariably begin to rain—in horizontal torrents.

On the afternoon of the ship's departure it seemed as if the whole island was being evacuated. Men in oilskin jackets and high boots trudged past with crates and boxes. A World War II–era Land Rover and three tractors hauling trailers rode back and forth between the barracks and other buildings to the heliport, a concrete red circle separated from the monument to the dead by a few overgrown gardens.

Thirty passengers from the *Marion Dufresne* and fifteen residents climbed into the helicopter in groups of four. Once again the administrateur was the first to leave, along with the mailbags. He waved farewell like a king to his subjects. Fifteen men said good-bye to their colleagues who were staying behind, and to the island where they had spent a year and a half; some of them were crying. When the last passenger was in the cockpit, the pilot made one final sweep over the heads of those left on the island before return-ing to the ship. Then the horn sounded, and after fifteen minutes the *Marion Dufresne* had completely disappeared from view.

Suddenly the only sounds that could be heard were the surf and the hoarse barking of the fur seals. The wind was gaining strength. Without a word, thirty-six men walked back to the settlement and disappeared into their barracks.

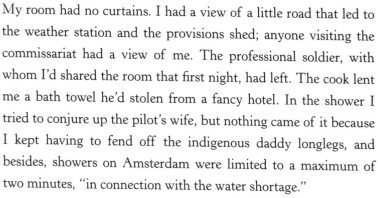

My room had no curtains. I had a view of a little road that led to the weather station and the provisions shed; anyone visiting the commissariat had a view of me. The professional soldier, with whom I'd shared the room that first night, had left. The cook lent me a bath towel he'd stolen from a fancy hotel. In the shower I tried to conjure up the pilot's wife, but nothing came of it because I kept having to fend off the indigenous daddy longlegs, and besides, showers on Amsterdam were limited to a maximum of two minutes, "in connection with the water shortage."

I lay down on the top bunk and took out the biggest notebook I had. I drew up a kind of calendar for my stay on the island, showing the weeks until the return of the *Marion Dufresne*, and crossed off the first two days.

As small and remote as the settlement was, it had the air of a genuine capital. Civic institutions included a volunteer fire company, garbage collection service, hospital, department of "public works," power plant, workshop, water purification station, mechanical garage, weather station, open-air slaughterhouse, communications center, and various laboratories. There were vegetable gardens, a narrow lane lined with flower boxes (the boulevard Martin-de-Viviès—the only street with an official name), a few side streets, a small square with two trees, and a little spinney called AmsParc.

The Great Skua housed the dining hall, the kitchen, the video room, and the library—a single room that had photos of old missions on the wood-paneled walls and damp books from the 1950s on the shelves. There was even an open-air swimming pool, but this didn't seem to have been used for years: A fur seal had fallen in and met its death on the tiles below, where it lay, partially gnawed-on and in an advanced state of decomposition.

There were many facilities, but few personnel. Thus the district chief also hunted cows and exterminated rats, and the Chimney was not only doctor, veterinarian, dentist, and surgeon, but also the garbage man, dishwasher, psychologist, cleaner, and shopkeeper.

Amsterdam proved to be a land with neither keys nor money; the Chimney sold his cigarettes and bottles of whisky on credit. Soap, caps, and rolls of film were always in stock, but he did not sell cookies, gym bags, Scotch tape, books, or chocolate in any form. The Chimney hated the role of shopkeeper, and was particularly averse to selling shoes: "Feet always stink so much."

Almost immediately after the *Marion Dufresne*'s departure, the tone of the settlement changed. The meteorologists urinated unabashedly against the walls of their own office. Most of the newcomers stopped shaving their faces and started shearing their heads. For haircuts they went to the Slaughterer, a Creole from Réunion, who served officially as butcher and assistant cook and, more informally, as masseur and gardener. In his capacity as barber he offered three styles, which happened to coincide with the three settings on his electric shaver: perfectly smooth, practically bald, or visible stubble. The drying room in the Tern, two houses down from me, functioned as his barbershop. After I first witnessed him in action, I dreamt that he had decapitated me with a machete and cut me into pieces with a circular saw.

Four days after the *Marion Dufresne* set sail, it was Christmas. We drew lots and exchanged packages containing comic books, condoms, rolls of film, girlie magazines, and chocolate bars covered in white mold. I gave one of the aerometrics experts two bottles of Beaujolais, which I had bought aboard the ship. The package under the Christmas tree addressed to me had a bottle of shampoo for dull and lifeless hair. The cook managed to silence his critics with an elegant Christmas dinner, for which he had dipped deep into his stores: terrine of sole with Amsterdam chive butter, roast turkey with chestnuts, and pineapple.

The Ascetic played accordion and the Singer entertained the crowd with sentimental love songs all night long. I stood on a table and sang "Ne Me Quitte Pas." Then the four members of the local rock band plugged in their guitars and improvised a performance that lasted several hours.

Bonbon was the lead singer. With a cigarette in his mouth he moaned unintelligible Lou Reed lyrics into the microphone. He had been given his nickname by the helicopter pilot's wife, who had compared him to the heavy baby sea elephants that the killer whales would toss into the air like beach balls before gobbling them up like so much candy. Bonbon proved to be a tireless initiator of parties, fishing competitions, and barbecues. He had signed a contract for six months on Amsterdam; after that he planned to move to Honduras: "I bet it's beautiful there, too."

The band played on through the night, even though most of the people gradually wandered off. At four o'clock in the morning I walked to the overgrown gardens by the monument to the dead. The seals were barking; it was humid. Suddenly the clouds opened up and the moon cast a halogen-like glow over the ocean. I heard snatches of music; the air was heavy and salty. I looked up at the sky: The stars were overwhelming; the moon among the splotchy clouds. Nothing is more liberating than self-imposed solitude.

At my request I was soon able to move from the Sheathbill to the Tern, one of the two barracks that were nearest to the shore. My new neighbors across the lane—Stéphane, Bonbon, the Cyclist, and the Slaughterer—had a panoramic view of the pier and the ocean beyond, while our group—the Marathon Runner, the Greek, René (who was secretly called Pigpen), and I—looked out onto a little grove of phylica trees and the back of the Petrel barrack.

My new room was empty, so I brought along some furniture from the Albatross: a very low table that must have done duty in a French classroom some thirty years ago, and a desk chair with a sticker that read: Southern Lands, #834/3540, not intended for consumption. When it rained outside, it would leak inside. The barracks reeked of fur seal and dampness.

The Mosquiteer was supposed to come by in "a few weeks" to install the screens; until then I had to put up with swarms of blue blowflies. The Biosol, a gangly youth from the Alps, explained to me that the flies were such a nuisance because there are no insectivorous birds or other natural enemies on Amsterdam. That was also why they showed no flight reflex. Moreover, being well adapted to the strong winds, they would not let themselves be blown off your hand. The flies mainly fed on fur seal and cow carcasses. "There is no natural balance," the Biosol had said. "Everything's getting totally out of hand."

There was an indefinable tension between the new arrivals and the members of Mission 48 who had stayed on after almost a year and a half on the island. The newcomers could be subdivided into the "vacationers," who would only be spending the summer, and the winter crew, or "hibernators," who formed part of Mission 49. Other lines, too, could be drawn: between soldiers and civilians, between professional soldiers and conscripts, between conscripts and scientists, between young and old, between rookies and Amsterdam veterans, between old and new school aerometrics specialists, between radicals and conservatives, and among the meteorologists as a group. But all of these fundamental distinctions faded when the *Marion Dufresne*—together with the helicopter—sailed away and we realized we were stuck with one another. The island didn't even have a boat of its own: "Where would you go?" the district chief had said. "The nearest land is nearly two thousand miles away, over the roughest seas on earth. Where are you going to go to get help?"

Amsterdam had no history, at least not in the sense of stories, ideas, or illusions that had been passed down from father to son, aunt to niece, or neighbor to neighbor. In this sense the island had no tangible past. Nevertheless, this obvious lack of permanence was counterbalanced by an unconscious, imperceptible progression as the veterans passed on customs to the new arrivals. Thus

Mission 49 continued the practice of scraping a dinner knife against a plate whenever someone showed up late for dinner. Certain habits evolved over years or even decades. One such custom was the "Heurtin moment"—a period when people simply sat there without saying a single word. The expression referred to a family who, in the 1870s, had made a spectacularly unsuccessful attempt to settle permanently on the island.

I was just a temporary resident, still in unfamiliar territory. But because the history of the island was rewritten with every new expedition, I was just as much a part of it as any other inhabitant of the earth who had ever set foot there. Yet at the same time my presence seemed to be inherently meaningless: In a few years no one would be left on the island who knew me or even knew that I existed. It gave me an uneasy feeling; I always like to leave my mark on things.

Life in the capital proceeded at a slow pace, the tranquility of the streets broken only by the sight and sound of men urinating— using the toilets for that purpose was forbidden. Most movement took place at twelve fifteen in the afternoon and seven thirty in the evening, when the meal bell would ring and the residents of Martin-de-Viviès would come running from all sides. After nine o'clock in the evening the island seemed dead.

We all shook hands every day. I learned that even if someone had dirty or wet hands, you were still expected to touch him, even if by taking hold of his wrist. It was impolite to skip somebody, but it was equally inappropriate to shake hands with someone you had already greeted earlier that day, since that meant you had forgotten the first meeting. In the morning the men ate bread that had been removed from the Deepfreeze and allowed to thaw, covering a slice with chocolate spread and dunking it in a cup of lukewarm instant coffee. Officially breakfast was served from six to nine, but after eight forty-five you ran the risk that the resident "maid of the day" would have already started taking out the garbage pails and tossing the dining hall chairs on top of each other.

The first few days saw a lot of parties. The meteorologists, the soldiers, the hunters, the conscripts, the glaziers—everybody had get-togethers with the other members of his own group. This reinforced my need for seclusion.

"On this island you've got two kinds of people: those who unconsciously look toward the False Peak, and those who keep their backs to the hills," said Clammy. He was a short meteorologist, who would stand two inches away from whoever he was talking to and then lean in closer when his interlocutor recoiled at the first bit of spit.

I understood what he meant. You had people who looked to security, who reveled in the island's visible finiteness; and you had others whose eyes were always fixed on the horizon. I belonged to the latter group.

I often carried around a list that depicted the diving sequences of the five species of whale that could be found in the waters around Amsterdam. It also showed pictures of their spouts, taken from various angles. Residents were expected to record any sightings in a notebook in the library. I was once with Louis, who was looking at the Lower Venus Crater, his back to the sea. Suddenly he turned around, pointed at the water, and said, "Look, a killer whale." I never saw anything special myself. To my mind, Amsterdam seemed enveloped in an oppressive sameness. Ships rarely passed by, not even in the distance. During the past year no one but the Singer had even seen an airplane, and that was too high to be heard. I had already heard him tell the story twice: the first time during the banquet with the administrateur, and later at the bar of the Great Skua.

The realization that I was almost certainly the first Dutchman to stay on Amsterdam for an extended period of time excited me, especially during the first couple of days. No one on Amsterdam understood the essence of that sensation; for them, the island was just another part of France that they called "Ams" or simply "the base." Even the brochures and books in the library usually began their histories of Amsterdam with the first time a *Frenchman* had seen the island: That was in the eighteenth century, and the man didn't manage to make it ashore. Only one book referred to the oldest exploration of the island, but even there the French authors wrote of "Wilhelm van Vlaming," instead of "Willem de Vlamingh."

During the last days of December it rained constantly, but on New Year's Eve the skies finally cleared, despite a stiff and cold south-easterly wind. I had picked up a dry cough, for which the Chimney had prescribed a throat spray. The medicine was a year beyond its use-by date, but the doctor-in-residence didn't consider that a problem: "You can go on using most medicines even after the expiration date. It's not as if I really have a choice. It takes forever for my orders to get from Paris to Réunion and then all the way back here. Besides, a lot of the pharmacies see Amsterdam and the other Southern Lands as a good place to dump old stock."

On New Year's Eve the Great Skua was decorated with streamers and balloons. With the help of the Slaughterer, the cook had put together an elaborate buffet. In no time the men began singing sea shanties at the top of their lungs and fighting their way through the assortment of wines and champagnes. The atmosphere was festive, even boisterous, and after a while nobody minded Clammy's pushiness. To my surprise, some people went to bed before midnight, although the Dreamer explained to me this was "not unusual in France." At midnight, on the little street in front of the Great Skua, I wished him and Louis a happy new year. After that we stopped talking and looked at the stars.

Where were the others? Louis nodded in the direction of the video room. I walked back inside and opened the door to the annex of the main building. In the dark I could make out at least ten men—each one sitting in the middle of an otherwise empty row of chairs—watching a hardcore porn film on the big screen. I joined them for a short time, but the panting noises blaring out of the speakers made me uncomfortable. I walked back to the Tern. Outside, everything was quiet and isolated, as always.

Amsterdam had its origins in an enormous volcanic eruption along the fault line of three continents that had drifted apart after the ice age. As the glaciers and pack ice were slowly receding, the sea level rose, submerging more and more of the original crater; a series of brutal explosions had blown apart the west side, which was now largely washed away.

The island was nothing more than an extinct volcano with the peak lopped off, resting on a steep base surrounded by oceanic troughs several miles deep. Underwater, Amsterdam was connected to Saint-Paul, almost fifty miles away, but that "blood relationship" had never done much for either island.

No man had ever seen Amsterdam when a nation on the edge of southern Europe began to probe, confront, and eventually pass beyond the bounds of the earth. It was these Portuguese seamen who permanently debunked the prevailing conception of the world as an island surrounded by a limitless ocean that gradually merged with the "Heavenly Dome."

Europeans had never sailed past Cape Non, on the west coast of

Africa. Beyond that was "the Realm of Satan"—a land of scorching heat transected by rivers of fire. South of that began "the Green Sea of Darkness," the domain of monsters who could devour whole ships, a place enshrouded by thick fog that blended sea and sky.

The little nation of brash seafarers first attempted—very cautiously—to sail past Cape Non. Once they succeeded, the world was open to them. One of them remarked, after journeying to the ends of the earth, "We discovered new islands, new lands, new seas, new peoples, and what is more: a new sky and new stars."

It did not take long for them to reach the southern tip of the hot continent, which they eventually named the Cape of Good Hope. After that they set an easterly course and sailed farther and farther into the unknown. They sailed more seas and saw more islands, mountains, and rivers than all previous seafarers put together.

The Portuguese explorer Fernão de Magalhães had a vision that would bring him eternal fame. He was firmly convinced that somewhere in the New World discovered by Columbus there was a passage; if he could only succeed in navigating it, he would be able to complete the greatest voyage ever dreamed of, the culmination of all the crossings of the previous centuries—the first journey around the world. Magalhães was from the only part of his country where the ocean could not be seen. Unloved by his countrymen, he had defected to Spain. As Fernando Magellan, he succeeded in winning support for his project from the king and from the queen mother, Joanna the Mad, who spent most of her life locked up in her castle.

On August 10, 1519, 5 ships departed Seville, with 265 men on board, as well as 95 dozen spears, 1,000 lances, 12 hourglasses, 508 bottles of wine, 200 barrels of sardines, 984 cheeses, 7 cows, and 3 pigs. After a year and a half of searching, the Italian, Greek, Maltese, Spanish, Portuguese, German, African, and English desperadoes who formed the crew finally found the passage that would become known as the Strait of Magellan, between the extreme southern tip of South America and Tierra del Fuego. But by that time they had already lost two ships—one to desertion—so that only three of Magellan's fleet sailed into the infinite void, the yet unexplored waters of the Pacific Ocean, where no white men had ever ventured before.

This new world had no coastlines and proved to be infinitely larger than they had imagined. The hardtack began to spoil; the drinking water turned yellow and started to stink. The sailors were forced to eat sawdust, rats, and dried oxtails. By the time they finally reached the Philippines, after three months and twenty days at sea, nineteen of them had starved to death.

The discovery of new land meant food and fresh drinking water, but also catastrophe: During a battle with the natives, Magellan got a lance through his forehead and was hacked to bits. During the next leg of the expedition two of the three ships were lost. The surviving crew members, reinforced by some twenty captured natives, continued the journey crammed aboard the puny *Victoria*, the smallest and most vulnerable ship of the original five. Terrifying monsters were painted on the bow of the *Victoria*; images of saints hung in the cabins. The crew had elected as its new captain the Basque Juan Sebastián Del Cano, who had begun the expedition as commander of the *Concepción*. For weeks on end he followed a southerly course, without quite knowing where he was or where he was headed.

By then the majority of the original crew had either succumbed to disease, drowned, deserted, or died in fights, so that only forty-seven sailors and officers remained. They had robbed, killed, raped, and pillaged, but at night, by the light of the moon and the stars, they said their prayers, begging for forgiveness and a safe return. In the oppressive vastness they crossed the southern Indian Ocean, where no human being had even been before. Although they had taken five months' worth of provisions, mainly meat, they had not been able to salt it adequately, and it soon began to spoil. Hunger and scurvy took their toll; the corpses were tossed overboard. The sailors had no reason to doubt what they saw, namely that the pagans immediately vanished into the swirling ocean while the Christians floated on their backs, their emaciated faces fixed on heaven.

The *Victoria* did not alter its course for a whole month. On March 18, 1522, the mate Francisco Albo noted in his log that he had observed high land at thirty-seven degrees, thirty-five minutes southern latitude: the island to be known as Amsterdam. They were unable to land because of the headwinds and the strong surf.

"We struck sails and waited until the next day," wrote the navigator. "The wind was from the west, we set our storm sails and headed north, against the wind. We were unable to shoot the sun. We sailed around the island left and right. It had a circumference of six miles and appeared uninhabited. On the twentieth—I did not shoot the sun—we departed, following a course northwest by north-northwest."

Those words are all that have come down to us about the discovery of the wayward lost island. The first people to get a glimpse of the formidable cliffs concluded that the place was inaccessible and insignificant and sailed on. They did not even bother to name the island after one of their saints. But they had seen it; it existed, and would be forever linked to the first voyage around the world.

Eighteen men eventually made it back to Seville, weak and ailing. They had been gone twelve days short of three years. In bare feet, dressed in rags and holding a candle, they did penance in the church of Santa María de la Victoria the day after their arrival. Inside the royal palace, the captain recorded the discoveries they had made, but he evidently thought the desert island at thirty-seven degrees south latitude did not merit any mention.

Toward the end of the seventeenth century, the Portuguese gradually began to lose their supremacy at sea; their position was usurped, at least in part, by another people living on the edge of the European continent: the Dutch. These traders from the North plied the Indian Ocean, bound for their archipelago in the East. The shortest route ran around the Cape of Good Hope and then northeast, straight across the Indian Ocean, but that course was plagued with lengthy calms. The sun was so hot that the provisions spoiled in the hold and the pitch melted in the seams of the ship. Captain Hendrik Brouwer was one of the first to attempt a more southerly route: It was a roundabout way to get to Batavia, but he had a westerly wind for twenty-eight days in a row and no calms. "There is no reason to fear running aground on a sandbar or shoal," he later wrote, "for we have found those waters to be one vast expanse of sea."

Not long afterward the new route became mandatory, and it was only a matter of time before Brouwer's supposition was disproved: Del Cano's nameless volcano was rediscovered, and from that moment it suddenly became part of The Great Circle—as the route to the East Indies was called: a solitary beacon along an empty stretch of water, nearly five thousand miles of open sea.

The island's destiny, then, was to be seen and avoided; it was an aid to navigation, but also an obstacle. Those who wanted to drop anchor were unable to make it ashore. But the island was no longer unknown; in fact, it was described with increasing frequency. "It consists of a small, round hill in the center and a large, high round mountain on the western side, which first appeared to be a separate cliff, but afterwards we found it to be part of the main body of the island; it is very high land; we observed few birds or other signs of life," Master Claes Hermansz noted in his journal in 1623.

Antonio van Diemen, who would ultimately name the island, set off for the East in 1633. He got off to a slow start. As a result of powerful headwinds, the *Nieuw-Amsterdam*, the *Oudewater*, and the *Veenhuizen* lay at anchor for eleven days at Vlissingen roadstead. A further delay of three days followed, when the commander contracted a "hard fever" and had to be brought ashore twice to be bled. Once the ships were underway, however, the voyage was not a bad one. From the time they left Texel there were only eight deaths, and because they were able to stock up on tamarind, plums, and oranges on one of the Cape Verde Islands, the crew managed to avoid scurvy entirely. They brought on enough pigs to slaughter one per day.

The three ships rounded the Cape of Good Hope and sailed without stopping into the infinite emptiness of the southern Indian Ocean. But near the point where São Paolo was marked on Van Diemen's map, the sky clouded over, and the ships got separated in the mist.

Saturday, June 18, 1633. Wind N.N. West with a stiff breeze until the middle watch. Very foggy weather, at times our visibility was less than three ships' lengths; no sun at dawn and no zenith that afternoon. God be praised, two islands have been sighted. We sailed between them and gave the more northerly of the two the name of Nieuw-Amsterdam Island, the other being St. Paulo. We had gone two months and twenty days without seeing land. We saw fit to hold our course for the southern coast of Java, unless weather and wind should compel us otherwise, God forbid!

The *Nieuw-Amsterdam* had sailed briefly past the high cliffs, and so Van Diemen had casually named the island after the flag-ship of his squadron.

The island Amsterdam retained its name, though it would suffer from a persistent identity crisis. Today it is no longer possible to say exactly how it happened, but from early on, British sailors called Amsterdam Saint-Paul and vice versa. This misnaming was reconfirmed in 1776 by the celebrated Captain Cook, and since one doesn't contradict a great explorer like that, the British went on confusing the names of the two islands on their nautical charts until well into the nineteenth century. The greatest victim of this stubbornness was the French captain François Péron, who in his memoirs had described his three-year stay on "Amsterdam," as the island was called by those on the American ship that had brought him there. In reality he had landed on Saint-Paul, which was not, contrary to his belief, even located in the Pacific.

With two other Frenchmen and two Englishmen, all of them sailors, Péron was taken to the crater—a natural harbor—with the understanding that a ship would pick them up in fifteen months. Péron had met his companions aboard the ship. On shore they proved to be ill-mannered drunkards, and Péron regretted the undertaking as soon as he saw the ship that had brought them sail away, but it was too late. "The most ominous thoughts racked my soul; I felt cut off from the whole universe, banished to a horrible wasteland and condemned to an exile, the magnitude of which I could not fathom," he later wrote.

The five men lived on a diet of sea elephant tongue, fur seal pups, petrels, and fish. The supplies soon dwindled, and the tensions among the island-dwellers mounted. In November of that year, Péron got into a blazing row with Godwin, an Englishmen whom Péron considered a good-for-nothing who had done nothing to help the group. During their argument, Péron pushed the Englishman into the crater lake. Godwin climbed out and, together with his countryman Cook, charged the French captain, hitting him with a stone, kicking him in the head, and stabbing him with a kitchen knife until Péron lost half his hand. He lay unconscious in a pool of his own blood until the two other Frenchmen finally succeeded in taking him away. The three Frenchmen escaped to the other side of the lake in a canoe while the British stayed behind, armed with a rifle, two pistols, a saber, and a sword. The unthinkable had happened: On an island of about four and a third square miles, a civil war had broken out. Three against two: French versus English, North Saint-Paul versus South Saint-Paul.

The French sought refuge in a cave, but they had no bedding; no extra clothes, bandages, provisions, fishing rods, or fire. The next day Péron decided to sail to the other side: "Courage won out over despair." The Britons allowed the three men to enter the hut they had previously shared and take tinderboxes, clothing, and a cooking pot. Later that afternoon the French spit-roasted a young fur seal on their side of the island.

The division of the island was a fact. The English raised their flag, and the French did the same. Péron devised a scheme to send one of his men, Gouju, whom he knew the British trusted the most, to the other side, claiming he had defected. Péron presumed that the rebels would welcome Gouju, if for no other reason than one extra man would give their party the clear majority. The plan was for Gouju to bide his time and then, when he knew that both Britons were unarmed, he would go to a predetermined location, take off his clothes, and wave them in the air. The goal was to capture the cabin, because whoever controlled that, ruled the island.

Two months later, the time was ripe. Gouju gave the agreed-upon signal, and Péron and his colleague rowed across the lake. They took the two Britons by surprise and forced them to grovel and beg for forgiveness, which Péron then granted, ending the war of Saint-Paul Island. The Britons were banished to the cave, and from then on they had to have Perón's permission if they wanted to go anywhere.

But the ship that was supposed to pick them up did not come. Gouju fell ill and died. The remaining four had spent a total of three and a half years on Saint-Paul when a ship finally appeared on the horizon. "It was on a day that I was sitting at Gouju's grave with tears in my eyes. Gaudin was standing next to me when he suddenly cried out, 'A ship, there, a ship!' " Péron later wrote.

A British captain approached the island in a canoe. He was willing to give the four survivors passage to his next destination, but he had no room for Péron's twenty-seven hundred neatly dried and stacked seal pelts.

Amsterdam, for its part, resisted any encroachment on its freedom from the day it was discovered: It was uninhabited and belonged to no one. Fear and greed were the motivations of the first people who set out to rob the land of its independence. Hoping to beat out their powerful British rivals, thirty Frenchmen headed to an island to which they had no legal right but which they were nevertheless determined to claim. On July 1, 1843, the three-master *Olympus* dropped anchor off the coast of Amsterdam; Captain Martin Dupeyrat and a garrison of twelve men under the command of Louis-Adam Mieroslawski succeeded in rowing ashore. With some effort they managed to plant a flag in the rocky ground. At the foot of the flagpole they buried a document stating that Amsterdam had been claimed "by order of the governor of Bourbon and in the name of France, in the presence of the members of the garrison, who presented arms and performed the customary homage."

Months later the captain of a passing French provisioning ship concluded that France would gain little from a permanent occupation of Amsterdam and Saint-Paul, due to the inadequate living conditions. The French king subsequently refused to ratify the claim and re-called his garrison. But fifty years later France took a step that would have a lasting impact on the island's history.

It was on a dismal spring morning in 1892 that the reconnaissance ship *La Bourdonnais* headed for Amsterdam, with official orders to establish dominion over the wayward island once and for all. As soon as the False Peak came into view, it began to storm, forcing Captain Vuillaume to point toward the open sea and sail close-hauled, tacking around the island as best he could. In the course of the afternoon he ventured a bit closer to the shore, but the surf was so rough that a landing party was out of the question.

Surely a mighty empire like that with such a refined culture and such mighty soldiers could capture a tiny island that had no other means of defense than those bestowed by nature. In the hope of eternal glory, the first mate and two sailors shed their uniforms and leaped naked into the waves. They managed to avoid the submerged rocks and reached the lava strip on the northeastern side of the island. They had brought a line, which they first made fast to a rock, and then used to haul ashore the necessary attributes for the claim. On a base that spun around like a weathervane, they mounted a well-tarred flagpole that sported an iron flag: Amsterdam Island had been taken once again.

Later they would proudly describe to the authorities in Paris how they had risked their lives so that Amsterdam could be added to the empire, but their candor had a disastrous effect: A claim made by three men, naked and sopping wet, could hardly be sanctioned. Therefore it was decided that the ceremony should be repeated as soon as possible, this time with the transport-reconnaissance ship *Eure*.

On January 25, 1893, a few dozen sailors and officers stormed the island of Amsterdam, with all the documents necessary to establish their claim packed in a waterproof envelope and sealed in a case. They buried the case, put up a boundary marker, and set down a block of oak with a copper plate engraved with *Eure—1893*. For future castaways they left thirteen casks in a cave, containing thirteen hundred pounds of corned beef, eleven hundred pounds of hardtack, ten flannel shirts, ten pairs of woolen underpants, ten blankets, and a few canisters of matches.

The sailors lined up next to the iron flag and presented their bayonets to the ship's gun. Lieutenant first class Delzons, surrounded by his officers, declared that he was claiming the island in the name of the Republic. The bugler played "Au drapeau!" and from the reconnaissance ship came the roar of twenty-one cannon.

After that the men launched their dinghies and left with the *Eure*, heading in a southerly direction. The ceremony had gone off without a hitch, though on that very same historic day *La Bourdonnais*—the ship that had made the first, unsuccessful claim—went down with all hands in a cyclone in the waters off the coast of Madagascar. There was a party on board the *Eure;* the ship's cook served roast sheathbill, preceded by fresh penguin soup. Amsterdam had been "conquered" and added to the French Empire forever, although on the face of it nothing had changed. More solitary than ever before, the island sat there in the emptiness of the ocean, having lost its function as a beacon long before the French finally staked their claim: With the opening of the Suez Canal, ships very seldom passed those latitudes.

The uninhabited island in the Juan Fernández Archipelago that served as the setting for Daniel Defoe's *Robinson Crusoe* had in reality been used for decades as a penal colony—a fate shared by many of the world's most remote islands. It was virtually inevitable that Amsterdam would be destined for the same purpose.

At the end of the eighteenth century, the British discussed the idea of incarcerating their worst prisoners on Tristan da Cunha, while "the cruelest and most intractable among them" would be sent to Amsterdam, which at that point had yet to be claimed. The French authorities, too, considered the Southern Lands suitable for "hastening repentance"; they saw Amsterdam as an ideal place "because of the very healthy climate." However, none of these plans were realized, and the island remained uninhabited for more than a hundred years.

In the course of the twentieth century, Amsterdam's location suddenly became a matter of strategic importance. Warships from various countries had been exploring the surrounding waters, so in order to secure the island from foreign invaders, France decided to take a decisive step: Amsterdam would be given a permanent capital.

In late 1949, the lobster boat *Sapmer* skimmed past the dark belt of sheer cliffs that protect Amsterdam from the outside world. On board the ship were five meteorologists, four radio operators, and a male nurse, who, together with a team of Malagasies, would become the first residents of the new settlement.

"Between the gray of the sea and the gray of the sky, a promontory comes into view, scarcely any darker than the vague horizon. 'That had to be it!' "—wrote the leader of the expedition, Paul de Martin de Viviès, in his journal.

The mountainsides are dotted with old craters; the cones themselves have been more or less preserved. The bluffs slant down at a precipitous angle, providing just enough room for a sloping,

inaccessible beach littered with gigantic boulders and, a little
farther, a chaotic, uninviting patch of ground. Nevertheless it
seems that this is the only place where we could possibly disem-
bark. The binoculars eagerly scan the coastline. A strip of lava
holds back the surf that pounds the shore: that will serve as our
landing. But then?

Their first attempt to come ashore was unsuccessful because of
bad visibility. The next morning the sea still seemed too rough, but
the surf was a bit calmer near the anchorage by Dumas Crater, so
that the men could jump onto a rock by timing their landings
between waves. In this way a number of men made it ashore, bringing with them two light tents, provisions, tools, and explosives.

They determined that the lava tongue was the only place suitable for unloading large material. The problem was that this natural "pier" had a tendency to disappear into the churning sea at the
slightest rise in surf. So they had to level off the jetty and carve an
escape route through a moraine of enormous rocks—all with the
help of dynamite. That day the air was filled with the echo of four
hundred exploding charges; hundreds of penguins and fur seals
fled. Four men stayed on the island that first night.

The heavy use of explosives recalled the Allied landing at Normandy—a resemblance that was reinforced by period equipment
that included inflatable rafts, jeeps, and even a narrow gauge rail
on which the heavy crates were hauled uphill by hand.

Four days later, a wave hit a raft carrying several members of
the expedition, hurling them against the rocks—a bad omen. They
all fell into the sea, but escaped uninjured. On the eighth day of
the disembarkation, the inevitable happened. One of the rafts,

which was still not fully loaded and therefore was unsteady, was moored alongside the lobster boat when a high wave caused it to capsize. The twenty-two-year-old sailor Emil Ribault went overboard, taking with him a load of thirteen hundred pounds of sheet iron. The accident happened at a place where the floating algae had roots that went down over forty yards. The young sailor was never found; the attempt to subjugate the island had claimed its first victim.

On January 26, 1950, the eighty-eighth and final raft landed on the pier. All in all, the Malagasies had safely ferried ashore more than two thousand crates, losing only fifteen to the sea. At first the tents stood a few hundred meters from the lava tongue, but soon the road was laid, and the camp could be moved to the site of the permanent base, thirty meters higher. The first barracks were constructed. A photograph hanging in the library of the Great Skua shows the capital in its infancy: the French flag in the center of two rows of barracks—a street plan that essentially hasn't changed in fifty years.

The new inhabitants of Amsterdam were plagued with sow bugs and blowflies, which they tried to eradicate with DDT. They deployed a cat they had brought from France to exterminate the mice. The cat, in turn, was terrorized by penguins, who did not appreciate his overtures; later, the cat was attacked in one of the barracks by a large Amsterdam wildcat. One of the meteorologists managed to trap the beast under a footstool; after that he struck the animal on its head with a bottle and strangled it with a belt. The inhabitants of Amsterdam unanimously decided to eat the wild cat the next day, but they never got that far. "Its blood had been drained; it had been cleaned and marinated, but in fried form, the smell of the meat alone was enough to take away any desire to consume the animal," wrote the expedition's leader De Viviès.

Two events marked the growth of the capital: the baking of the first baguettes, which brought an end to the diet of war bread that they had been subsisting on for months, and the construction of an administrative center, the first office in the Southern Lands. A hurricane made one last attempt to torpedo the permanent occupation of the island, but beyond inflicting some damage to the barracks, blowing over the antennas, and completely destroying the last vegetables that had tried to grow there, it didn't do any harm.

In this way Amsterdam became a district capital. Soon a weather station sprang up, and with it, a center for radiotelegraphy, although the connection with the "Ministry of State, responsible for the Sahara, the overseas departments and territories" seven thousand miles away was regularly disrupted for long periods of time "due to holes in the propagation of the radio waves." "Hello Amsterdam Island, this is Paris! Do you read me? Over!"

The pioneers were not relieved until thirteen months later, when they were replaced by a group that called itself "the second mission." The island had four chiefs—of the district, the weather station, the radiotelegraphy station, and the engineering corps—and an array of service personnel: handymen, a gardener, a dishwasher, and two bellboys.

New barracks were built, as were a system of water pipes, an electrical network, a signpost, post office, garage, town square, seismological station, and hospital. The city was expanding, and the first victims of this expansion were the rockhoppers. These little penguins abandoned their colony that was closest to the settlement, although whether they did so of their own free will is disputable, as the new human inhabitants raided their nests for eggs, which were used to make "anemic, but not unappetizing" omelets, and developed the habit of stuffing birds as souvenirs.

Today, nearly fifty years after its founding, the capital of Amsterdam bears the traces of long vanished hope. Everywhere I went, I saw remnants of gardens, which someone had once planted and tended, and which now were succumbing to the wind or the neglect of later inhabitants. The duck pond was empty, the greenhouse bare except for a single tomato plant; half the chickens had returned to their feral state and were living in the fur seal colony. The cabin that had been named after the drowned sailor Ribault was falling apart, even though the packaging tags were still stuck to the front door; the carpenters' and plumbers' workshops were no longer in use.

Nothing symbolized these illusions better than the experimental windmill, which had lasted less than a year. In the old photographs it looked like a giant eggbeater on legs. Of course, if there was one thing that Amsterdam had no lack of, it was wind, but the gusts proved to be so powerful that the moorings had given way and the eggbeater launched itself into the air. The blade had disappeared, but the blueprints were still on display in the ruins of the foundation. The Chimney, who considered himself a "fundamentalist Catholic," was working on a plan to convert the old windmill into a chapel. The result of an earlier attempt to keep the population of Amsterdam in the grip of the Mother Church could be seen on the outskirts of town, in the form of a reinforced concrete floor that was to be the basis of a church. But Paris had put a stop to the project when it turned out that the selected holy site seriously disturbed the seismological readings.

Thus every improvement, each new initiative that was taken on Amsterdam had a tendency to fall victim to the elements, and disappear as if it had never existed: Clotheslines blew away, flower stems snapped off, and the three passenger cars that had been shipped to the island rusted beyond use in less than six months. It was an island in a permanent state of decay, beaten into submission by the elements, defenseless against the dominance of wind and waves.

The outside world slowly receded from awareness. As soon as the *Marion Dufresne* left, the head of the post office took down the sign saying Next Collection. Yet the strange thing was that this didn't relieve him from having to empty the mailbox regularly. All residents had a right to telex eighty words a week, but most of them still preferred to write letters.

Officially Amsterdam was an international maritime radio station, but in practice the operators ignored any ships flying foreign colors. "Every once in a great while we see the contours of a container ship on the horizon, but if they're not French, we let them go. Besides, none of us speak English."

There was no television on the island; the only news available was a printout distributed by the radio personnel. Although it was known as the "World News," the report generally contained five-line domestic news items from the French national press bureau. A new copy was posted every week in the Great Skua, but I never saw anyone so much as glance at it.

One of the walls in the radio/telex center had a map that showed Amsterdam like a spider in a web of straight lines running to

Sydney, Antananarivo, Cape Town, and the South Pole. I saw it nearly every day, when I went to the annex for some freshly brewed coffee, which could be found there most mornings. Another wall map showed "The Southern Hemisphere," which, apart from a strip of Africa and the westernmost tip of Australia, consisted of nothing but ocean, interrupted by the occasional French rock—projections of a gigantic, invisible underwater empire: Amsterdam, Saint-Paul, Tromelin, Juan de Nova, Les Îles Glorieuses, Bassas da India, and Europa.

As Bonbon described it to me, Tromelin was a strip of French sand, just over a mile long and half a mile wide, to the east of Madagascar. The island had a flagpole and one building that housed two soldiers and two meteorologists. "A colleague of mine worked there for a year. They had a hurricane hit the island, and the whole place was covered with water. The four of them sat on the roof of the building for a week until they were rescued."

Amsterdam was the center of the world—at least according to the signpost at the start of the boulevard, which not only showed Paris, but also Los Angeles, Lima, Tokyo, Moscow, the Cape of Good Hope, and Calcutta. In view of the immeasurable distance between these destinations and an island that didn't even have a rowboat, their presence on the sign attested to a boundless optimism—possibly even to a certain arrogance. Of course, the list of faraway places could also be interpreted as a somewhat desperate measure to help cope with the surrounding emptiness.

As the new year got underway, the subgroups began to intermingle, though the line dividing the forty-eighth from the forty-ninth mission had by no means disappeared. Veterans of the earlier group continued to look askance at the newcomers, whom they saw as interfering with their own established norms and customs. They seemed unable to accept the dissolution of their former community, as well as the inevitable erasure of all signs of their group's shared past, once they left the island. In vain, they tried to pass on certain rites and rituals, such as their manner of publicly correcting someone by slowly raising one's hands to a shouted crescendo of "Hooooo-eee!" So in time they gave up on that, just as they abandoned their opposition to the fact that Bonbon and the Dreamer would openly flout regulations by drinking after hours— 8:30 P.M.—in the bar of the Great Skua.

I mostly talked with the American—a French glazier who lived in America—as well as with Louis, the Dreamer, Kaplan, and Longhaired Nico, all of whom could look forward to another year and a half of Amsterdam. Once, the Dreamer showed me his personal domain—the small shed and two cubicles where he recorded geomagnetic and seismological data. On average, a minor earthquake hit Amsterdam once every three years. "It's no big deal," said the Dreamer. "In fact, nobody would pay any attention at all if it weren't for the fact that three tectonic plates come together right here at Amsterdam."

In his small laboratory he showed me the latest readings from the seismograph located fifty miles away on Saint-Paul. The instrument's arm was moving frenetically up and down. I looked at the Dreamer quizzically.

"It's been like that for a few days now," he said. "It may mean nothing, it may mean everything. It could be a sea elephant rubbing up against the meter, a rat chewing on the cable, a bird that's built its nest around the instrument. But it could also be a volcanic eruption or an earthquake on Saint-Paul. And in that case, the tidal wave is already headed right here. There's no way for me to know. Our instruments cover a large part of the world; we can pick up every little tremor in Tokyo, the South Pole, or in Siberia. But we have no idea what's going on fifteen miles away. That's just how it is: The closer the meter, the more inaccurate it is.

I soon discovered Radio Ams. I had tuned to the local FM station during my first week, but all I could hear was a constant, indistinct drone. I learned from Louis that the radio transmitter was located in the Alley, a cul-de-sac between the kitchen and the freezers of the Great Skua. Radio Ams turned out to be nothing more than a CD player. The CD that had been selected was skipping, so I rummaged through the disorganized pile and chose five new albums. I put them in the carousel, selected "Random Play," and pressed "Start." The broadcast was resumed; the program would repeat itself until someone else replaced the CDs I had chosen with something else.

One dry day I sat down on a mossy hill, as I often did. I outlined what I wanted to research about the island's history, and I wrote in my diary. To break the silence of the island I turned on my Walkman. I was aware of my tendency to suppress my feelings by trying to rationalize and explain things away, by shrugging my shoulders, by eating candy bars, or by getting high. But what good did it do me to know all that?

Just before leaving for Amsterdam, I had had an intake session with a psychotherapist.

"What's your primary feeling at this moment?" she had asked.

"I'm feeling pain. And anger," I had answered.

"I see you have your arms crossed and that you're looking away from me," she said. "What are you thinking about?"

"About how I'm going to a coffee shop the minute I get out of here to buy a joint and how after that I'll go home and smoke it."

"If you do that, our conversation today will have been pointless."

After the session I walked by the coffee shop but didn't go inside, and went on for a walk in the park instead. But then I wound up buying a joint, anyway, on my way back. Why not? I figured.

I stared at the sooty albatrosses circling the east shore. Amsterdam was cut off from the rest of the world in an almost violent way, but that was exactly what I liked—the tangible sense of boundlessness that surrounded the island. I checked my watch: time for lunch. Generally speaking, people on Amsterdam didn't keep track of the time. After all, even just to spend two days on the island, you had to pass at least five weeks at sea—and this wasn't counting the time you needed to fight your way through all the red tape. And if you wanted to stay any longer than two days, you had to spend at least two months. Days turned into weeks without anyone seeming to notice. But there were certain times during the day to which everyone paid attention: lunch at 12:15, dinner at 19:15, quiet at 20:30.

Anyone planning to spend more than a year on the island had to undergo a psychological exam to prove to the medical department of the Southern Lands that he could endure "prolonged confinement in a male environment cut off from the outside world."

Some of the men had been kicking around the Southern Lands

for years. The absolute record holder was the Slaughterer, who had been working on Amsterdam for twenty years, taking turns with his brother, who came to relieve him every six months. A community had evolved of men addicted to the oceanic desert, a small society of those who had spent large parts of their lives on Crozet, Kerguelen, or Amsterdam—without being allowed to settle there permanently. For a glimpse of their world you can turn to *Friends of the Southern Lands,* a periodical published on the mainland, which runs photos of men in shorts on snowy mountaintops, tables of minimum temperatures, logs of storms, displays of stamp-covered envelopes, announcements of incomprehensible ministerial decisions, and obituaries.

When the first weather station became operational, signaling that the permanent French presence had become a reality, the highest-ranking administrators of the Southern Lands issued an official proclamation banning women from the island. But that was rescinded several years ago, and although for some time they continued to advise women against a two-day visit—on the grounds that this would "confuse" the local population—this warning, too, has been repealed. Nevertheless, no woman has yet been invited for a longer stay on Amsterdam.

A similar situation existed on Crozet, where no women had been stationed for over four decades, until the administration of the Southern Lands changed their policy. On board the *Marion Dufresne* I had met a soldier who had been stationed on Crozet for a year and a half. "During my time on the island, there were five women out of a total of twenty-five inhabitants," he had told me. "One of them was married and therefore unavailable. Two of the girls quickly found steady boyfriends, but the other two had relationships with a number of men. That didn't work out so well. The scientists were suddenly at each other's throats, and we saw some pretty hefty fights break out."

Almost all the barracks and labs had a wide variety of pinups prominently displayed among maps of the world and photographs of albatrosses or high-pressure systems. As the departing district chief had told me: "Out here, women are reduced to the purely physical. There's no show or tell about girlfriends. What goes up on the walls are bare tits, not love letters."

In the screening room of the Great Skua I watched a video of the forty-fifth mission that showed two men performing a fantastic imitation of an albatross couple in full strut. Now and then some of the residents would don wigs and dresses from the costume trunk for a party. But weight lifting, too, was a popular pastime. Men like Clammy and the Marathon Runner liked to go fishing at 4:00 A.M. in force ten winds and wore shorts even in the coldest weather. But the American topped them all one day by diving off the pier into the churning sea, stark naked, "just to freshen up."

I had managed to borrow two sets of bedsheets; I'd bought a skating cap at the store; I'd even gotten hold of some paper clips so I could put my papers in some semblance of order. Frequently I withdrew to my room to read or write, even though the musty smell from the damp walls refused to go away. Evidently no one complained about their living circumstances, about having to spend months or years in a tiny room about six feet by six feet. "The Southern Lands administrators could care less if the rooms leak; they're mostly concerned about maintaining their own positions," said the American. "The soldiers and the scientists doing their government service have to keep their mouths shut, and everybody else gets bought off with extra premiums."

Now and then I'd wake up in the middle of the night to the sound of moaning, but I never knew if it was the wind or my neighbor, Pigpen. For a long time I held on to the hope that I'd eventually be able upgrade my room to one with an ocean view, but one day I realized no one would be leaving and no one new would be coming and everything would stay the way it was.

The weather was often dreary, even now that it was summer. It rained nearly every day, and the storms sent strong gusts sweeping through the capital. In actuality these downpours were little more than a brief break in a very short cycle; the island seemed to have no soil, so the rainwater seeped straight through the porous rock back into the sea. There were a few pools, but the ones on the shore were full of seals or sea elephants, and the others were either inaccessible or very temporary. Our tap water came from what was collected in the gutters, which was then purified.

It turned out that one of the reservoirs was leaking, and the Singer, who had already banned the use of flush toilets for urinating, now ordered us to save on water generally and curtail toilet use even further. "Preferably two or three visits a week, and certainly not several times a day," he announced once during dinner, cutting off all protest. "It's very simple. If everyone follows my advice, everything will be fine. If not, we'll run out of water in three weeks."

I performed my chores without grumbling: mopping the floors of the Tern; disinfecting the communal shower and the toilet. In the

Great Skua I dried the dishes almost every night; I played chess and foosball. As the year progressed, I stopped counting the days until the arrival of the *Marion Dufresne:* I had finally become an inhabitant of the island of my dreams.

Amsterdam was part of France, and the inhabitants formed a cross-section of French society: technicians and soldiers, university professors and men who had never gone to school, Parisians and villagers, Basques and Bretons, whites from Europe and Creoles from Réunion. In exchange for cooking lessons, the Dreamer taught the Slaughterer to write; the Cyclist seemed to regard me as a walking English dictionary. In return he showed me his scrapbooks, which contained all the finish photos and newspaper clippings for the 304 races he had won in as an amateur cyclist.

The professional soldiers always sat together at mealtimes in the Great Skua, as did the meteorologists and the aerometrics specialists. Only the district chief carefully rotated his place, choosing a new table every day, and even a different seat. I had no regular table, but I preferred the scientists or meteorologists to the professional soldiers. Most of the time I didn't have a choice: The sound of thirty-six scratching knives and one empty seat meant I was late for dinner once again.

The cook made an effort to serve a different main course fourteen times a week. The men were generally amenable to anything, as long as it wasn't spicy; the one time the Slaughterer replaced the cook and "oriental langoustines" appeared on the table, ten of the men refused to serve themselves.

Sometimes there was tough talk, such as when the cook threatened to confiscate the remaining cheese unless we stopped cutting such big chunks; when the district chief reminded us once again that we were supposed to let him know in advance if we planned to leave base for more than an hour; or when the forty-eighth mission complained about the poor quality or even the total lack of desserts, "which we had gotten used to with the previous cook."

It was an unwritten rule that you didn't bring up other people's pasts or their lives on the mainland; the outside world was far away. At the table the men talked about recent discoveries—a new sea elephant; a rare kind of bird vomit or unexpected penguin tracks; or an abrupt change in weather. Sometime they would sing a French song about "a young woman of ninety who liked whipped cream, though she hadn't creamed in years," all the while banging their fists on the table. Personally I preferred a fifteenth-century drinking song in which the King of England was doused with "a bucket of shit."

In the past, the "boys" from Réunion would serve the gentlemen scientists and soldiers, but budget cuts during the 1970s had put an end to that, and the inhabitants of Amsterdam now had to do their own dishes. Anyone who didn't help dry or put things away was given the cold shoulder. The result was that there were always too many of us in the kitchen, jostling one another to get our hands on a plate; the one time I avoided kitchen duty, I felt guilty.

I loved evenings and nights on the island, especially when there were no clouds and the ocean took on the color of the milky white moonlight. Amsterdam had little artificial light; the capital had more rain gauges than streetlamps. Outside the settlement it was pitch black. There were two beacons mounted on the north side of the island; the other shorelines were cloaked in darkness after sun-down. When it wasn't raining I'd often walk in the dark to the overgrown gardens near the helicopter pad. There I listened to the barking of fur seals and tried to be happy.

Every Saturday the dinner tables were cleared away and the telex operators would show 16mm films, which, according to the credits, had been "approved by the ministry." There were dubbed West-erns from the fifties, and propaganda films from the Cold War, with lots of jet planes flying in formation over oceans, coasts, and cities. Their wings were painted red, white, and blue, and the jets released smoke in the same French tricolor. Lyrical voices sang the praises of French hegemony and the heroic struggle for parity on the high seas.

During the rest of the week, some of the men retired to their rooms right after dinner, while others played foosball or read in the library. The professional soldiers in particular made use of the screening room: After they had exhausted the assortment of dubbed American action films, they made their way through the porn collection, which they maintained themselves, trading with the sailors on the *Marion Dufresne* four times a year to acquire new material.

Some decades earlier, the soldiers had once decided to segregate themselves completely from the civilians. "Soldiers are used to a commanding officer," said the district chief. "They can't take the fact that there's no hierarchy on the island." For some soldiers the island was nothing more than a halfway point in the sequence Mururoa, Sarajevo, Abidjan. The Greek, on the other hand, had spent four summers on Amsterdam without ever feeling the need to leave the capital, except when his work required it. But the greatest contrast was the one between the opportunists and everyone else. The opportunists were the ones who duly performed their chores—putting in windows, reading barometers, or recording the atmospheric acidity—but viewed their prolonged isolation as a necessary evil they needed to endure in order to be eligible for special bonuses.

Others surrendered to the primal force of the island. They climbed Mount Dives and the Great Balcony; they sought the seclusion of Cape Vlaming; they made the punishing trip from the Cathedral to Cape d'Entrecasteaux. They studied the landscape, which had no pretensions of being anything other than what it was: a piece of earth whose past had been blown away by the winds. They explored every hill and photographed every lost phylica tree, every newborn seal among the rocks, and every new nest of the Amsterdam albatrosses. They knew that no one was allowed to settle permanently on Amsterdam, and most of them realized that it was very unlikely they would ever return. For that reason their love for the island was irrevocable and unconditional.

Several decades had passed since Del Cano first discovered the island, but at the beginning of the seventeenth century, Amsterdam finally began appearing on world maps—though it was sometimes depicted south of Romeiros Island, which often bore the caption "may disappear depending on the level of the tides." However, like other islands such as Jesus, Roggeveen, Indépendence, and L'Enfant Perdu, Romeiros was eventually removed from the nautical charts because it turned out to be fictitious.

The first sailors who actually set foot on Amsterdam came from a country whose greatest thinkers were gripped by doubt. The Dutch passionately disagreed with one another on issues such as whether the earth revolved around the sun or vice versa, and whether God had really stopped the sun for an hour at Joshua's request as the Bible stated: "So the sun stood still, and the moon stopped, till the nation avenged itself on its enemies."

Whatever their disagreements, these God-fearing merchants still dominated the oceans; they exploited their colonies, built great sailing ships and impressive houses with stepped gables. They adhered to the Scriptures even though some of them denied the existence of devils in general and Satan in particular. During their Golden Age, they accumulated more wealth than anyone had ever thought possible. But then, slowly but surely, came the inevitable decline. The cities became depopulated; purchasing power decreased, and the Amsterdam Stock Exchange fell into the hands of speculators. The Dutch Republic began to go to seed.

In November of 1695, the Dutch East India Company decided to send one last expedition to the Terra Australis—a mission prompted by the disappearance of two ships: the *Vergulde Draeck,* which had been gone for forty years, and the *Ridderschap van Holland,* which had vanished more recently. The latter ship had set sail from Vlissingen and had been last seen at the cape. If the ships hadn't run aground on the coast of the Terra Australis, there was one possibility where the marooned sailors—if there were any—could be found: "The islands of Saint-Paul or Amsterdam, which are said to lie right in the middle, as it were, of the route to the East."

"Calling upon God to bless all our endeavors," the Heeren XVII (Lords XVII), as the board of directors was known, decided to place the leadership of the expedition in the hands of "a most capable person"—Willem Hesselsz. de Vlamingh, from the island of Vlieland, who had just returned from a voyage to Greenland as the commander of *D'Hoop op de Walvisch.* For this new undertaking he would be paid the sum of eighty silver guilders a month.

Dutch ship logs have little positive to report about the island of Amsterdam. Whoever approached the land had to contend with strong currents, stormy weather, drizzle, fog, or "thick air." For that reason it was often impossible to shoot the sun. Ships' masters tried to avoid landing on the island, because the shoreline was too steep, the water was clogged with "some kind of duckweed," and the entire island was surrounded by rocks both over and under the water.

De Vlamingh was ordered to split up his squadron, sending one ship around the island to starboard, and another in the opposite direction. He was to fire his ship's gun every half hour to prompt a reaction by any castaways: "be it with fire, smoke or in some other fashion." Should he find any survivors from the *Ridderschap* or any other ship, he was to offer them the necessary provisions, and "if their number be not too great," was obliged to take them on board as passengers. De Vlamingh and his crew were also to be "vigilant in searching the area for the remains of any ships."

It had not occurred to the Heeren XVII to order De Vlamingh to actually lay claim to the island; after all, Dutch merchants had controlled the sea route to the Orient for almost a century. They had seen the island's peak loom on the horizon countless times, and they had given the land its name. Now the only important question was what, if anything, did Amsterdam have to offer? What sort of harbors and bays could a ship find there? Or were there too many dangerous "sandbars, rocks and shoals?" Was there shelter? Water? What sort of trees grew there, what sort of vegetables? De Vlamingh was expected to investigate all these matters on site and submit a report of his findings, illustrated with "good, accurate maps."

De Vlamingh was given command of three ships: the heavily armed frigate *Geelvinck,* which served as flagship, and two smaller three-masters, the hooker *Nijptangh* and the galliot *Weseltje*. A total of nearly two hundred crew members were recruited, especially "unmarried and determined" men who could not be of "the papist religion or accused of any crime." In addition to masters, mates, boatswains, sail-masters, and sailors, the muster roll lists soldiers, carpenters, fire tenders, and water mates.

After a short delay—just out of Amsterdam the *Nijptangh* hit a sandbar off Pampus—the squadron left Texel roadstead on May 3, 1696. The next day, assistant carpenter Cornelis Ewertsz came down with a "great blockage in the lungs accompanied by a bad cough." He was also bringing up bloody phlegm and ached in all his limbs. A mixture of crab eyes, antimony oxide, and tincture of opium brought him back to health. The German sailor Willem Aentreder was not so lucky. He died after a few days at sea. After his death the surgeon discovered "a yellow-green matter" on his foreskin, and concluded that the patient had succumbed to "the French disease."

Fearful of French pirates, De Vlamingh decided to avoid the Channel, and sailed around Scotland with a convoy of whalers. The squadron passed the Shetlands and reached the Faeroe Islands—the northernmost point of their journey. After that they changed course to head south-southwest, and eventually south.

The ship's bill of fare consisted mainly of peas, beans, cheese, and pickled meat. Piglets and chickens had also been taken on board. One problem was the drinking water, which turned murky and started to stink of hydrogen sulfide through contact with the wooden barrels. The stores of vegetables and the fruits also spoiled quickly.

More crew members fell ill. Water mate Jan Laegeman succumbed to dysentery; quartermaster Pieter Matiesz was found dead in his bunk, "after having been carried there following a night of excessive drinking." Sailor Ditlof Schoenmaker caught "the pleurisy" on his right side. The surgeon had six ounces of blood drained from Schoenmaker's arm, and prescribed a diet of ship's beer, bread, and soft-boiled eggs, but the sailor soon died despite the cure. De Vlamingh noted in his journal: "Sailor Schoenmaker from Lübeck died toward nightfall; wind at night S.W. and S. with a topsail breeze till morning."

At night all movement on deck lessened considerably, with just the sailors on the middle watch, who had to turn the hourglasses every half hour, even in the worst weather. They knew not to try to shorten their shift by turning the glass ahead of time: "eating sand" was punishable by death.

The crew prayed to God for favorable winds. They all knew stories of ships that had been blown off course by storms and set to drift across the ocean, as the crew watched their food stocks dwindle away. There were even cases where the threat of starvation led to some of the living being thrown overboard, to save provisions. And although it was of course taboo, everyone knew that in some dire emergencies the officers and sailors had resorted to cannibalism, beginning with the passengers, who, when all was said and done, were nothing more than "cargo," followed by sailors in irons and the cabin boys.

High seas and rough weather met them off the coast of Tristan da Cunha. Seaman Luytie Jansz's legs broke out in purple lesions, and his gums turned "black and rotten," according to the surgeon, who twice cut out the diseased tissue and instructed the patient to rinse out his "most fetid mouth" with horseradish wine and essence of scurvy grass—everyone knew what that meant. Pneumonia, edema, and scabies also began to take their toll.

Four months after their departure from Texel, the three ships reached the Cape of Good Hope, the crew filthy and fatigued. There had been eight deaths, and twenty-one sick sailors had to be admitted to local hospitals. "Thank the Lord God that we have had a safe journey thus far," wrote De Vlamingh in his journal.

Laurens Zeeman, commander of the *Weseltje,* died at the cape. The crew was unable to find a suitable replacement, as there was no one on shore with any experience in sailing a galiot. Willem de Vlamingh proposed his son Cornelis as the new captain. The boy had left Texel as third mate on the *Geelvinck,* and he was only eighteen years old, but "quite experienced in the art of navigation." The governor of the cape, who had to approve the appointment, deemed it "not inexpedient" to entrust Cornelis with this responsibility, considering that he was "a sober and vigilant lad" who could be expected to "assist [his father] more loyally than anyone else."

According to various reports, the coasts of the Terra Australis were populated with "barbaric and cruel savages"—reason for De Vlamingh to take along "three shackled Negroes, who were knowledgeable in a variety of tongues and native to the area around the South Land." They were to help De Vlamingh communicate with Southlanders or other people they came in contact with.

It took seven weeks before the sick men recovered and the ships were reprovisioned. The dead crew members were replaced; sheep, goats, castrated rams, and crates of fruits and vegetables were hoisted on board the ships, and by order of the governor of the cape, the men were supplied with a week's supply of fresh bread prior to signing on.

On Saturday, October 27, 1696, the three ships left on the trail of the missing *Ridderschap van Holland.* Departing the cape so late in the season was actually against company guidelines, which instructed "outbound East India ships" to weigh anchor no later than the end of September, so as to profit the most from the west winds "along the customary course of 38 to 40 degrees."

"God grant us good fortune and a safe journey," wrote De Vlamingh. He had started out as a whaler, but in his new job he had to play many roles: astronomer, geographer, adjudicator, soldier, merchant, visionary. He needed to possess an undaunted yearning for the unknown. He was required to be a keen judge of character. Above all he had to trust his own instincts and take charge without hesitation, even if his sailors and the officers threw up their hands in despair, fearing themselves lost in the storms and darkness.

After rounding the cape, the three ships sailed in a convoy, off into the emptiness. The days were monotonous: As far as the eye could see, there was nothing but high waves and water-laden banks of clouds. The weather ran from thick fog to drizzling rain to hail. One afternoon in mid-November, at a latitude of 39 degrees, 53 minutes, and an estimated longitude of some 61 degrees, a storm struck from the north-northwest; later that night what had begun as a light rain turned into a heavy squall, with pelting rain and dark skies.

Did the young Cornelis feel he had let his father down because he couldn't keep his galliot on course as the raging storm blew the *Weseltje* down to the fortieth parallel? In his journal, Willem de Vlamingh blames the deviation on the extremely high waves that threatened to wash over the ship—not on his son's inexperience. He himself managed to steer his flagship through the storm, with the *Nijptangh* in its wake. After the crew paused for their midday meal, the wind died down, and the captain gave the order to raise the jib and sail east. Later that day the three ships were reunited.

A continent would be hard to miss, but the same could not be said for Amsterdam. Although the location of the island was known, finding a tiny volcanic peak in the middle of five thousand miles of open sea was no easy task. And while the East India traders had sighted the speck of land on a number of occasions, they had just as often sailed right past without noticing it, whether because of hail or thunderstorms, or because the False Peak was hidden by patches of fog. The same could easily happen on a clear day; all it took was a slight mistake in navigational reckoning. On the Mercator map aboard the *Geelvinck*, Amsterdam was charted at approximately 38 degrees to 39 degrees southern latitude, and 95 degrees longitude, but the mapmakers cautioned that that a ship might "encounter the aforementioned island much earlier than these estimates indicate, as the bearings could be off by as much as a hundred miles."

According to De Vlamingh's calculations, the island of Saint-Paul could not be very far off, and on November 25, he conferred with the commanders of the other two ships, after signaling with flags. In his log he wrote: "Spotted a seal. 87 degrees longitude, with foggy weather."

On November 27, exactly a month after departing from the cape, he recorded "a flock of crow-like birds." That same day, the chief surgeon on board the *Nijptangh* noted: "Four glasses into the middle watch, we saw seaweed floating in the water; the crew was issued their first rations of olive oil. Toward evening several small tuna were seen." And the following evening, before sunset, he wrote, "During prayers we again saw drifting seaweed; De Vlaming fired the ship's gun and unfurled the flag, to signal that land had been sighted, said land being St. Paul. We sailed eastward and saw the land E.S.E. of us." Four Spanish reals were paid to the German sailor Pieter Mathijsz, as he had been the first to see land and shout, "Land ho!"

The harbor of Saint-Paul was, according to De Vlamingh, "as good as that on the Cape of Good Hope," with no swells, and a shore that was mostly safe to windward. The next morning after breakfast he sent the dinghies onto the island. The men found "so-called sea lions"—"though these creatures look nothing like lions, being some twenty feet in length." The sailors knocked the animals unconscious with a stick or shot them twice in the head, "after which we sat down to smoke a pipe-full of tobacco."

The men brought aboard a dinghy full of "sea bream, cod, Hottentot fish and large lobsters without claws." Then, "seeing that there was nothing more for us to do on the island," the squadron left, four days after arriving, with a west wind that kept up till morning.

The crew hadn't even finished their morning prayers when they saw Amsterdam looming north-northeast of the ship: a round volcano with a truncated peak, the higher slopes covered with an apparently impenetrable belt of rushes, reeds, shrubs, and ferns. The island seemed inhospitable: The menacing, precipitous cliffs on the western shore looked like bulwarks designed to protect the island fortress from the constant, merciless gales that came from that direction. The surf thundered against the few beaches they could see, giving an unwelcoming impression. The current was strong and unpredictable. But in the end, the island offered little resistance to being opened to the world: December 3, 1696, dawned dry and clear, although the wind was so fierce, no sails could be carried other than the topsail. As the ships made their way around the island, the crew saw seals everywhere, which made "a tremendous din." On the *Nijptangh* the sailors caught a sea bream, which was "quite tasty."

"Monday morning, the wind from the W., off the coast of the island Amsterdam. Sent the hooker and the galiot round the N-side of the island, and our ship sailed along the S-side, where we found some occasional good anchor-ground," wrote De Vlamingh. Closer examination, however, revealed that the south side was full of rocky shoals and too shallow for De Vlamingh's frigate. He gave the first mate orders to cast the lead from the rowboat, in order to find a place for the ships to drop anchor. The man soon returned, after having found "black sand-ground," sixteen fathoms deep, at a distance of one cannon shot from shore. The *Geelvinck* fired two shots, and the *Nijptangh* and the *Weseltje* came alongside and dropped anchor.

Perhaps De Vlamingh had become too much a man of the sea; perhaps at this stage in his life he considered land anathema. Whatever the reason, he casually passed up the historical opportunity of being the first man to set foot on Amsterdam, leaving that honor to his assistant and bookkeeper, Joannes Bremer, from Copenhagen: "Sent the boat to take our bookkeeper ashore."

Taking a Greenland skiff, Bremer and a number of sailors went out to look for a suitable place to land. The traditional welcome prayer was the last thing on his mind; they hadn't even brought along the customary gifts for natives—wine and a pig. Amsterdam was uninhabited, they were certain of that, and there was no trace of any castaways.

We will never know who was the first to clamber over the slippery rocks and reach the shore, more than 144 years after Sebastián Del Cano had discovered the island. Was it the Dane Bremer, or some unknown cabin boy who fearlessly leaped into the sea to cut down some troublesome rushes and kill the most aggressive fur seals so his superior could get on with his work without being disturbed? Both De Vlamingh and the chief surgeon failed to record that information.

By early afternoon, Bremer and his team were back on board; they reported to De Vlamingh that there were many seals on the island and they had had to kill "a host" of them that were "in the way." Bremer had seen many thickets and trees, the trunks of which were as thick as "a man round his middle." With great difficulty they had made their way through the woods and the dune grass in search of fresh water, but despite a lengthy hunt, they had found nothing.

Later that day, De Vlamingh decided to go ashore after all. His most important discovery was that "there was as much firewood as anyone could want or desire," a good thousand shiploads' worth.

. . .

Meanwhile, the master of the *Nijptangh* reported shallow, rocky ground on the north side; the sea was rough, but he had spotted some fresh water at the point where the land began to slope away. So the next day, De Vlamingh sent another party to scout for water on foot, and ordered his son Cornelis, the first mate of the *Geelvinck*, and Bremer to row around to the north side, where waterfalls had been sighted the previous day, to look for a possible place to land. Their verdict was negative; the north shore could not be attained without great difficulty and grave danger: "Only the most dire need of water could induce one to land here."

As he had done on Saint-Paul, De Vlamingh had a number of fires lit on Amsterdam, "to determine if there were any people." Cannon shots reverberated along all sides of the island, but apart from that, the place was still. A few crew members were sent to the south side in a dinghy to look more closely for wreckage of the *Ridderschap* or any other ship, but one look at the vertiginous cliffs dashed any hope. Inspection of the other shores also yielded nothing. "The men reported seeing no remnants of shipwrecks, or anything else, for that matter," wrote De Vlamingh.

That same afternoon, the master and the chief surgeon of the *Nijptangh* once again went ashore. For any future castaways they sowed barley, peas, and mustard seed at six difference places, "in good ground, with soil to the depth of three feet, and below that a type of stone resembling charred pumice; on the whole the earth was peaty, richer in some places than in others, and free of vermin." They found holes in the ground and many dead birds. "Our men caught a weasel and two gray hares." They also came across a vegetable that was similar to wild celery, which proved to be edible. They found the ground to be "very loose," which they deduced was the reason why the trees on Amsterdam were so low, "as they were unable to send forth sufficient roots into the ground."

Meanwhile, the *Geelvinck* had sailed around the island with another mission. On board was one Victor Victorsz., whose official duty—according to the ship's roster—was to tend to the sick, but who had primarily been recruited to draft charts and make accurate paintings of the "the land, reefs and sand, troughs and shallows and any unusual things they might encounter." For all his duties, Victorsz. received thirty guilders a month.

Early on the third day, after morning prayers, De Vlamingh summoned the masters with signal flags, and set their departure for that evening. A dinghy was sent ashore one last time to gather plants and "a few branches from the sizable, linden-like trees," which were abundant. The thicket, too, "could be seen from a distance of one to two miles." The sailors also took some seal pelts on board and caught enough cod, bream, and lobster to fill an entire ship.

Toward evening all men reported back to their ships. "After having searched the island carefully and found nothing other than what has been reported, we resolved, in the name of God, to weigh anchor and set sail and continue our voyage to the South Land," wrote De Vlamingh. Amsterdam had shown its mildest side: three days of calm weather. On its way to sea, the anchor of the *Nijptangh* hung up on a rock and could not be raised. Was it possible that the island was attempting to hold on to its first visitors just a little while longer? De Vlamingh brought the *Geelvinck* to the galliot's aid, and it took ten hourglasses for the crew to pry the anchor loose using a windlass.

De Vlamingh had a wooden sign placed "half-way up the mountainside" bearing the text: "The ship DE GEELVINK, 1696, Master Willem de Vlaming, with the hooker DE NIJP-TANGH and the galliot DE WEESEL, bound for the South Land, Anno 1696, December 3." He hadn't actually claimed the island. The little monument made no mention of his reasons for landing; he had even left out the island's name. Vlamingh was clearly bound for other destinations, and Amsterdam was no more than a way station—an impenetrable island with no harbor or shelter, of little or no interest for his employers. So in the end, Amsterdam was left behind, as it had been for centuries: groaning under the force of the western winds and hidden by patches of fog.

Some two years after his departure from Texel, De Vlamingh returned to Holland, "elderly and frail." It was not a happy homecoming. The mayor of Amsterdam, the driving force behind the expedition, wrote, "Little has been gained from this expedition, as the commander was given to drink, and though he did sound the coasts, his search of the land was over-hasty, preferring, as he did, to while away his time at the Cape with much feasting and merrymaking, which was, to my mind, a most regrettable decision." Although he later toned down his judgment of De Vlamingh's efforts, the mayor remained disappointed by the results of the voyage. Though the captain had fulfilled the nautical aspect of his mission, he had found no trace of the *Ridderschap van Holland,* and had only visited places where no profit was to be made. Nor had De Vlamingh managed to "lay his hands on a Southlander, either by purchasing one or finding a volunteer, and bring him hither, where he could be taught the Dutch tongue, so that he might report on all he had seen and heard." Two or three times the crew had seen "a few naked Negroes from a great distance," but the latter had run away. The ship's supply of trinkets had proven to be useless, so De Vlamingh had to hold a public sale in Batavia, where he suffered a loss of 795 guilders (bearing the imprint of the Maid of Holland), 5 stivers, and 8 pennings.

The logbooks and journals of the three ships' captains were copied, reviewed, found to be in order, and filed away. We know nothing about De Vlamingh's later life. It seems that his only accomplishment was to definitively refute his own hypothesis that high winds made debarkation on Amsterdam Island a practical impossibility.

To Willem de Vlamingh, Amsterdam had seemed like one great forest, but little remained of that now. Three centuries after human feet trod first upon the moss, nearly all the phylica trees were gone: cut down, trampled by wild cows, or burned. At this point only vestiges remained, known as the Great Wood, the Old Grove, and the Lone Tree, scattered around the foot of the bare slopes, sole witnesses to a pristine past.

"The forestation was so dense it was impossible to cover more than four miles a day, forced as one was to crawl through the bush and climb over the trees," De Vlamingh had written. I wanted to feel what he had felt. On an overcast but windless day during the first week of January, I strapped on my backpack and set off for the phylica forest. It was an hour's walk, but the trip was perfectly safe, and you were allowed to go there on your own, as long as you told somebody in advance. Leaving the capital, I set off east, to the accompaniment of some ethereal American voices from the CD in my Walkman.

I opened the gate of the "first cowline," one in a series of partitions designed to protect the capital from an invasion of wild cows, whose presence on the island was the direct consequence of an optimist's illusions gone awry.

After De Vlamingh's expedition, fishermen and trappers had begun visiting the island. Seafarers on their way to the Great South Land also dropped anchor there to stock up on firewood and drinking water, occasionally searching for lost ships, castaways, or hidden treasure. They looked around, plundered, and departed. For centuries, though, the island remained just a way station for those en route to more important destinations or on the path to eternal glory. But there were two people, two dreamers for whom Amsterdam itself was the goal to which they had pinned all future hopes, a farming couple by the name of Heurtin. Accompanied by four farmhands, he, his wife, and their three children sailed from Réunion to Amsterdam on a large fishing boat, which dropped them off on the uninhabited island in January 1871. The weather was cooperative, and they managed to get everything ashore: livestock and seed, building material, children, and servants.

Starting from nothing, they began to construct their settlement, building a farmstead out of wood and reeds. The four servants lived in the rear of the house, which looked out onto the Elephant Pool, while Heurtin and his wife had a view of the sea. They planted vegetables and kept cows, pigs, and chickens.

Heurtin had a dream of Amsterdam as a southern Normandy, full of apple trees and undulating hills with grazing cows. But the pasture was such that the cows stayed scrawny, and the harvests failed because of a lack of soil and too much wind. The solitude, too, was oppressive, and the family yearned for home. Their food supplies dwindled, and two servants died. After less than a year, the settlers were on the verge of a collective nervous breakdown. Famished and demoralized, they managed to attract the attention of a passing fishing boat. Without looking back, the Heurtins left the island, never to return.

Two years later a British captain was given orders to look for castaways on Amsterdam, following a report that voices had been heard on the island. He found a flagpole and the Heurtin's deserted farmhouse. He saw nine beds and rolled-up bedding; cabin trunks with schoolbooks on history, religion, and literature; a section of a diary. It looked as if the Heurtins had run away without taking even their dearest possessions. The cabbage in the vegetable garden had gone wild. It would not be long before the farmhouse collapsed and fell prey to the west winds.

The most remarkable thing was that the five cows the Heurtins had left behind were all still alive. They had little drinking water or food; the slopes were too steep, the pastures too salt from the damp sea air, and the storms too severe, but apparently there was just enough moisture, food, and shelter to keep them from dying out.

From generation to generation, the descendants of those first cows adapted better and better to the conditions on the island. For the first few years, travelers observed that the cattle would voluntarily return to the stables. Later on the cows regressed to a pre-domesticated state and began to display the external characteristics of their aurochs ancestors, which had died out in the seventeenth century. They drank dew from the shrubs and grazed on tree branches; they stayed lean and ran up the slopes like goats. Their numbers increased steadily, even though many starved to death each year. They herded together and moved higher and higher up the mountains; their progress was slow, but after a century they had grazed more than half of the island clean. The ubiquitous cow paths cut across the high moorland, causing it to crumble away and disappear. The herds trampled the breeding ground of albatrosses and petrels.

Among humans, rats, and pigs, females tend to survive food shortages better than males, but on Amsterdam, the reverse happened, and in time there was an abundance of bulls. One of the reasons for this was that the long domestication had made the animals docile, in contrast to the aurochs, so the bulls rarely fought with one another. But the main reason for the imbalance was the lack of good pastures. During winter, the cows were in calf and at the same time had to nurse their previous year's offspring. They needed high-energy food, so they remained on the lower slopes. Meanwhile, the bulls and the infertile cows ventured into the highlands. The growth on the slopes was patchy, but that extra amount of grass and rushes was just enough nourishment for them to survive. It was the fertile cows that paid the price for their unrestrained reproduction: They died by the score.

In the 1980s, more than a century after the cows first colonized the island, catastrophe was imminent: The mass grazing had nearly exhausted the island's vegetation, and more and more slopes were turning into pools of mud. The herds were emaciated. The death rate among pregnant cows was higher than ever. The biologists intervened. They strung barbed wire across a distance of two and a half miles and shot all cows south of the fence. From then on, the cows' natural habitat was restricted to the northernmost part of the island, with the exception of the capital.

The original size of the herd had been cut down from two thousand to five hundred. In a bizarre kind of hunt, a few dozen animals—mainly bulls—were shot each year for food. A few pregnant cows were also shot, their fetuses removed and weighed for research purposes. The hunters stored the cow heads in the meat room, neatly labeled.

From the cowline I walked on at an easy pace. In ten minutes I reached Dumas Crater, from where I could see, in the distance, the peak of the perfectly concentric Grazing Zone. The path meandered along the Stone Quarry, which was used as a dumpsite for incinerated trash. The lava flows that led up to the crater were jet black and less than a hundred years old. Until a few years ago, Amsterdam had a dinghy in which the entire population could flee if the volcano should erupt. But one day a certain district chief—no one could remember which one—decided to have the dinghy removed. In his view it was just asking to be taken out fishing, exposing his men to the danger of being slammed against the rocks by a sudden surge. The district chief rightly calculated that the probability of this happening was infinitely greater than the chance of a churning stream of lava sweeping the inhabitants of Amsterdam into the depths of the ocean.

After the second cowline, a half hour's walk farther down, the path narrowed and the overgrowth became thicker. The island was at total peace. Below was the sea. On the shore I saw a swirling mass of white foam that hadn't yet recovered from the ravages of the last storm; it was dotted with thick layers of red and green algae, which faded into a grayish green before merging into the horizon. The Great Wood was located high atop Cape Rubble, at the foot of the False Peak. The moss- and rush-covered path led through the hills. The trees kept appearing and disappearing from view. I turned off my Walkman.

At the edge of the wood were cypresses, with the occasional eucalyptus—both planted to protect the last remnants of the primeval forest, still untouched but now smaller than a city park, from the storms. The remaining phylica had silvery trunks with the luster of an olive tree and the squat, bent habit of a mimosa. The species came from Tristan da Cunha, the only other place it was found. There, seeds had found their way into the stomachs of petrels and albatrosses, which vomited them up on Amsterdam.

A hallucinatory silence reigned inside the woods, coupled with the smell of fermentation. The thick carpet of yellowish and red-brown mosses had a sponge-like springiness. The phylicas stood clumped together in copses surrounded by rushes and ferns. Their black seed buds had a honey-like fragrance.

The phylica seemed downtrodden: twisted and oppressed. With admirable persistence the trees had braved storms as well as the cattle that before the arrival of fences had sought shelter in the forest from the occasional torrential rains. In the words of the Biosol, who studied the flora and insects, it was "good, homogenous wood with a strong structure."

The decline had begun with the moorland fires caused by fishermen and trappers, which sometimes raged for years, wiping out many of the man-sized ferns and rushes in the process. With that, the phylica lost their greatest protectors. All at once they were exposed to the full force of the winds that snapped their branches and snatched their fruit before it was ripe. The earth could no longer breathe, and the trees were threatened with decay.

I picked up a few seeds: They were oval, encased in shiny brown-black husks. The seeds contained nourishing endosperm, and for that reason they were a prized treat for sparrows, ants, timber beetles, and sow bugs—creatures with no natural predators on the island, which had come with Willem de Vlamingh and the hundreds who came after him. In time, these threats led to the worst disaster that can ever befall a flowering plant: The seeds no longer germinated. The symbol of Amsterdam, its only indigenous tree, was no longer capable of reproducing on its own. No young trees sprang up beside their parents, and the old trees died off. Generations of biologists tried in vain to coax the seeds to sprout.

That is, until 1974, when an agronomist discovered that the seeds of the phylica would germinate in boiling water. This led the way to a local phylica propagation program, and the replanting of dozens of new trees, particularly in the Great Tunnel and in the capital. But after some years these efforts were abandoned, and it is abundantly clear today that if the phylica is to have any chance of surviving, it will forever be at the mercy of its greatest natural enemy: man.

On my way back to the capital, I wondered if there could be any tangible evidence of De Vlamingh's visit: Was there anything left of the barley, the peas, and the mustard seed sown for future castaways? When I reached the settlement, I walked to the Biosol's shed and asked him about the local flora. The botanist showed me his herbaria, and a number of small pots with seeds and cuttings. I also studied the findings compiled by past resident botanists; the most recent overview listed all native plant species as well as forty-one introductions, primarily found on the lowlands. Eight of these new species threatened to overrun all the others. The slopes of Amsterdam were covered with saltbush, Queen Anne's lace, celery, mallow, hawk's beard, foxglove, dock, nasturtium, chamomile, and yarrow, but nothing remained of the seeds De Vlamingh had planted, according to the Biosol.

The sailors of the *Nijptangh* had been the only people ever to see a hare on Amsterdam. The weasel they had captured was likewise a unique event in the history of Amsterdam. To be sure, two centuries later, a French visitor did mention seeing "a small mammal, the size and shape of a weasel," but he hadn't managed to catch the creature. Neither his nor De Vlamingh's observation was ever confirmed, and no weasel bones had ever been found on the island.

Amsterdam was too remote for the autonomous presence of a small land mammal, the Biosol had explained. The sailors from the *Nijptangh* had probably seen the celebrated Amsterdam ducks, descendants of a flock that had inexplicably ended up on the island. These ducks had strayed too far away to fly back to the world they had left behind, and therefore had resigned themselves to spending the rest of their days on the island.

The ducks soon lost their ability to swim, and began evolving toward a sort of wingless state; over the centuries they developed into runner ducks that could dart through the rushes and ferns. Although they shrank in size somewhat, in general they had adapted to their new life with great success. They had no predators among the local animals, but in the end, centuries of castaways, trappers, treasure hunters, and lobster fishermen proved fatal to them, and today the Amsterdam duck is extinct.

Had De Vlamingh left no trace of his presence? What about the monuments he had placed on Saint-Paul and Amsterdam in 1696? Fifty-eight years after the plaques had been left, Godlob Silo, skipper of the *Drie Heuvels,* believed he had seen the last vestiges of them: "We found three to four pieces of firewood and a small piece of oak, likely the remnants of what Willem de Vlaming left here." But 250 years after Silo's testimony there was—naturally enough—nothing left.

Before leaving Batavia to return home, De Vlamingh had sent

the tangible results of his expedition on ahead aboard the ship 'S *Lanswelvaren*: a box of shells, fruits, and plants (which his employers judged to be "not particularly impressive"); a bundle of wood from the South Land with a bottle of oil distilled from it; a flattened tin plaque found on the island where it had been placed by Master Dirk Hartog eighty years earlier; and a sample of wood from the island Monij, "hewn from tall, heavy trees, which some think could be used to make ships' masts and seafaring vessels." The three black swans they had brought with them didn't survive any farther than Batavia.

Victor Victorsz.'s watercolors, which he had painted on folio sheets, were used for a few nautical charts, but they soon disappeared into the house of Claes Bichon, commander of the 'S *Lanswelvaren,* and they eventually found their way into the attic. There they remained until 275 years later, when two elderly brothers, direct descendants of the East India captain, brought out the trunk and donated the watercolors to the Prince Hendrik Maritime Museum in Rotterdam. In the collection were Victorsz.'s *Seven Views of the Island Amsterdam.*

"They had never been hung on display. That's what saved them," the woman at the museum told me. "Nothing is worse for watercolors." She had taken them out of storage for me to examine. "But they're fragile, which is why we don't exhibit them. They had been folded, so we opened them up."

The seven profiles of the coast had been painted in gray-green pastel tones, most of them from a distance of one cannon shot or a half cannon shot from shore. I told her about my research into the history of Amsterdam, about how frustrating it was that so few explorers had ever been able to land. "Not much is known about Amsterdam," the woman agreed. "Saint-Paul, on the other hand, is a different matter entirely."

I fell increasingly under the spell of Willem de Vlamingh. Where had he dropped anchor? And, more importantly, where exactly did the first person to land on Amsterdam—be it the unknown cabin boy or the bookkeeper Bremer—come ashore?

According to De Vlamingh, they had sailed along the south side of the island before the first mate found anchor-ground. And on watercolor 7, Victor Victorsz. had written in ink: "The Island Amsterdam appears thus when the peak is WSW from the observer; to approximately a short cannon shot from the shore, one finds a sand bar with black sand; this is the best spot to drop anchor."

It appears that De Vlamingh dropped anchor at Ribault, the anchorage on the north side named after the drowned sailor that was also used by the *Marion Dufresne*. But this wasn't entirely certain, since it is unclear what exactly Victorsz. meant by "the peak": Mount Dives or Olympus, which is now known as the False Peak.

Just like De Vlamingh, the painter and sick attendant Victorsz. never sketched or described where they ultimately came ashore. If they had chosen the current landing ground, why was there no mention of a "lava tongue" or natural pier in any of the accounts or journals? Another indication that De Vlamingh and his men might have landed elsewhere can be found in the Dutch periodical *Essays and Reports on Nautical Affairs, Seamanship, Hydrography, the Colonies and Related Fields*, from 1866:

When one approaches Amsterdam in the wintertime, one must proceed cautiously due to the strong prevailing winds, which are often accompanied by dark weather. The color of the water is not a safe guide and the northeasterly winds carry a great deal of seaweed. Anchorages are most likely to be found on the south side, since, it is said, the Dutch seafarer Vlaming anchored there in 1696. After that he is supposed to have come ashore and searched in vain for drinking water.

In any case, a more southerly landing was not out of the question, as was proven at the end of the nineteenth century by the British H.M.S. *Raleigh*, which made a successful landing a mile and a half southeast of the jetty.

My first goal would be Cape Vlaming, the island's southernmost point, which first appeared as such on a mid-nineteenth-century map, along with the note that "this name was already in use before our arrival." The map was a relic of an Austrian expedition designed to help acquaint Austrians with life at sea.

Evidently the name of the southern tip had been passed down from seafarer to seafarer and trapper to trapper as Cape Vlaming— without the "De"—until it ultimately found its way into the official French books. Could that be where the 1696 expedition had actually landed?

Hanging on a bulletin board in the Great Skua, next to the foosball table, was an overview of the expeditions that were on the program for that month, outlining the routes each one would take. Cape

Vlaming was nowhere on the list. "We never actually go there," said the Biosol, "But it's on the way to Cape Del Cano. I'm going there in about ten days to count thistles. You can come along if you'd like."

Although the hardest expedition was the one to d'Entre-casteaux—because of the obstacles on the way and the dangers involved—the longest and perhaps most exhausting hike was the one to Del Cano. I needed to do some training. I signed up for a number of day hikes; I had to get better at avoiding holes and learn to make my way through marshes with reeds several yards high. I had to learn the lay of the land.

The next morning I set out on my first big day-trip, to the Great Plateau, along with the Ascetic, Louis, and the Marathon Runner. We passed through the first cowline and climbed the Slope of the Wild Bulls. My rucksack was full: two liter-bottles of water, a packed lunch, an extra T-shirt, a thick sweater, a raincoat, a winter hat, gloves, a cap, and a flashlight with spare batteries.

The Ascetic carried the heavy apparatus that allowed him to maintain radio contact with the capital. Both biologists danced up the hill, and their caps gradually disappeared from sight. I could barely keep pace: My past of too many joints and too little sleep was catching up with me, and besides, the terrain was wet and rocky. There was no path until you reached thirteen hundred feet. The aurochs did not show themselves: They knew humans only as predators armed with prewar hunting rifles.

In the distance we could see the Dumas Craters and, closer by, Low Venus, High Venus, and the False Peak. Even at a thousand feet above sea level, Mount Dives could not be seen. We passed

Loulou's Hole, and after the second cowline we left the grazed land and followed the worn-down trail. The ground was strewn with slag, volcanic ash, and rocks with razor-sharp projections. Just before we reached the Great Plateau we put on our swamp gear: slick orange raincoats, and waterproof yellow waders that went over our jeans. These were held up by suspenders and taped shut at the tops of our rubber boots. After that we got down on our hands and knees and crawled along the trail like commandos. In reality there was no trail to speak of anymore, just a stretch of marshy ground; walking upright was impossible in the sucking mud.

Two great skuas followed us, feigning attacks to protect their nests. They looked like a kind of giant seagull but acted like true birds of prey, eating albatross and penguin chicks, petrels, eggs, and carrion. In a certain sense they were the true guardians of Amsterdam; along with the few sparrows in the capital, they were the island's only resident birds. They had a liberated lifestyle: *Ménages à trois* were not uncommon—sometimes a female lived with two males, or various females would share a nest with a single male.

At the foot of the Great Plateau we saw a bare hilltop come into view: Mount Dives, the tallest of the peaks. Then, to the right, we could make out Mount Fernand, a massive block guarding the west coast; on the other side of Dives were Mount Olympus and the Great Cooking Pot. On the plateau, the path again became passable. We walked through a disfigured landscape eerily reminiscent of the big bang: basalt blocks, small lakes, and secondary craters. The sodden soil smelled of decay.

Amsterdam is a solitary outcropping in an endless ocean located north of the point where the subtropical waters merge with the icy southern currents. The island's in-between position—between warm and cold, between equator and South Pole, between east and west—makes it an attractive meeting point for animals from the polar region, some of whom had evidently grown tired of always having to dive into icy waters, and preferred the relatively mild climate on Amsterdam. Some hundred thousand little penguins, seventy thousand yellow-nosed albatrosses, hundreds of terns, pale-footed shearwaters, soft-plumaged petrels, and sooty albatrosses would return every year to nest on the hillside and the cliffs: For Amsterdam, reproduction became a mass industry.

It was the island's remote location, more than two thousand miles from the nearest continent, that also furthered the evolution of new species among the animals that called tiny Amsterdam their permanent—albeit small—home. Three endemic petrels had become extinct, but a fourth species had survived, and Louis, the Ascetic, the Marathon Runner, and I were on our way to the nesting grounds of the rarest seabird in the world: the Amsterdam albatross.

For a long time this creature had gone unnoticed. The albatross lived in an area that was seldom visited and almost always obscured by clouds. In the summertime, birds resembling wandering albatrosses had been regularly observed on the Great Plateau. But for a long time no one found their nests, and for that reason they were initially thought to be some wandering albatrosses that happened to be incapable of reproducing. Then, in 1978, some members of the winter crew found five downy chicks, with no parents, and an ambitious biologist seized the chance to catapult himself into the world of ornithology.

The animal kingdom is dominated by invertebrates; the insects

alone have twenty times the number of species as all the verte-
brates put together. And half of the latter group consists of fish.
The chance of discovering a new species of bird was always
small, and has only diminished over the years. But three years
after discovering the chicks, the biologists found seven mating
couples of the new bird, a discovery that would change his life.
He followed the colony, carefully recording the differences between
these birds and the wandering albatross. He even proved that the
mating calls of the two birds were radically different in the upper
frequencies.

With its huge wingspan—over eleven feet—the wandering
albatross is the largest bird on Earth, but the Amsterdam albatross
isn't far behind, being just a little bit smaller, lighter, and darker
than the wandering albatrosses from which it had originated. To
establish conclusively that these were two different species of bird,
both birds had to be officially observed brooding at the same place,
without intermingling. Amsterdam wouldn't do, since wandering
albatrosses seldom went there, and did not nest on the island. But
the ambitious biologist was not about to let victory pass him by,
even though he would eventually have to share the honor with his
superior, who had sent him there.

Wandering albatrosses had never been observed breeding on
Amsterdam, said the two biologists. That fact in itself excluded
the possibility of crossbreeding with the new species they had discovered. Moreover, the brooding cycle of the Amsterdam albatross differed from that of its wandering cousins. According to the
ambitious biologist and his superior, the originality and the lack of
variations in the color pattern of the head and feathers attested to
the "reproductive isolation" of the population on Amsterdam, and

in their view the only possible conclusion was that the birds on Amsterdam did indeed comprise a separate species.

Their mission finally succeeded, and in 1984 the *Diomedea amsterdamensis* made its official debut in the history of evolution. Nobody made a fuss about the Big Exception, a couple consisting of a female wandering albatross from Crozet and a male Amsterdam albatross that had been living on Amsterdam for twenty years and regularly produced bastard offspring.

At one point the Amsterdam albatross had dominated the western slopes; its bones were found as far as the Antonelli Crater. Then came the seal trappers and, with them, rats, mice, and cats, all eager egg-thieves. But it was the Heurtin family or, more precisely, their livestock, that brought them to the brink of extinction. The wild cows trampled the rushes and reeds, crushed the mosses, and grazed the pastures bare, thus destroying a large part of their nesting ground. The Great Plateau was their last remaining bastion. There, the Amsterdam albatrosses could still find their favored habitat—low-lying, wet vegetation, reedy mosses, and marshy ground, and the constant west wind that kept them aloft when they sprang from the cliffs.

In 1991, in an issue of *Friends of the Southern Lands,* a former resident of Amsterdam attacked the ambitious biologist. The author claimed to have sighted the Amsterdam albatross years before the arrival of the ambitious biologist; as proof, he sent in a photo of a young bird, taken at the Vulcan Crater. He wrote that while he certainly did not presume to take full credit for the discovery—after all, these things depend so much on chance, anyway—it would only be proper to name the new bird after its true discoverer.

He didn't have a chance. The two biologists responded that the bird had been spotted shortly after the construction of the capital; what mattered was the scientific publication. And no one else disputed their claim.

At the time of my stay, a total of 130 Amsterdam albatrosses had been counted, 15 of which were mating couples. It was one of the only populations of birds in the world where each individual was identified annually. These were birds built for stormy weather: They could skim over the crests of enormous swells for hundreds of miles without flapping their wings. Their greatest foe, on the other hand, was the absence of wind; a calm could make them bob along aimlessly on top of the water. They never flew against the wind, and in clear moonlight they would fly all night long.

When they were old enough to leave the nest, the birds began a trek over the southern oceans and the continents, lasting about six years. And even though they only spent a fraction of their lives on land, they always returned to Amsterdam to find a partner and to mate.

We saw the first albatross, nearly full-grown and as big as a large goose. During a passing gust of wind he spread his wings, which seemed to be of prehistoric dimensions, and began to make flying motions. He was still waddling a little helplessly about the circular nest where he had been born, but he had already lost his down, and sensed that his departure for the seas was imminent. He did not panic at our approach. He was not afraid of man; he knew nothing of his ancestors' experiences with castaways or trappers, who roasted the birds on a spit and ate omelets made from their eggs.

According to Louis and the Ascetic, there would be ten young birds to track down, number, and weigh. They identified each animal individually, by means of a small metal ring around one foot and a plastic ring around the other. So the rarest seabird in the world was now on file, registered in a database for all posterity. Even on Amsterdam, human beings were flaunting their dominion.

An hour later I lay down in the enclosed depths of the Vulcan Crater. Behind me was Mount Dives, and in the distance, some five hundred yards below, the sea. The ancient cone sheltered me from the wind. Louis, the Ascetic, and the Marathon Runner had dropped out of sight; they were looking for nests near the Great Cooking Pot. The Marathon Runner would come get me in an hour. He had suggested we climb Mount Fernand together.

Above me was the approach route of the adult Amsterdam albatrosses, which whizzed by like gliders. Their colony might have been small, but it was healthy and no longer under threat of extinction. The death rate was exceptionally low, and albatrosses lived to an average age of eighty years. They seemed happy birds. It irritated me that the ornithological logbooks I had collected and lugged along on all my treks around Amsterdam tended to ignore any bird in the colony that wasn't part of a mating couple.

"What happens if their eggs don't hatch?" I had asked Louis. "Normally they lay an egg every two years, but the ones that are unsuccessful get a new chance after a year," he had replied. "If they still don't produce any young, they just keep on trying. They've invested so many years in each other it doesn't pay to look for another partner."

In the silence of the crater I thought about Saskia. I had broken up with her shortly before I left, although I still loved her. I took out the postcard with penguins I had bought in the Chimney's store.

Dear Saskia,

It's summer on Amsterdam, but the sky is full of clouds. I'm listening to the rustling, but not of trees. Because the island has so few, you soon get to know each one personally by touch—the rustling is the wind, which is slowly picking up strength.

We don't get a lot of fruit. I long for a crispy fresh apple. But also for the warmth of a body pressing against my own, for someone who loves me. From time to time. Or at least pretends to, if only it's pouring outside and we press our noses against the window and make love on the carpet in front of the gas stove.

In love, your A.

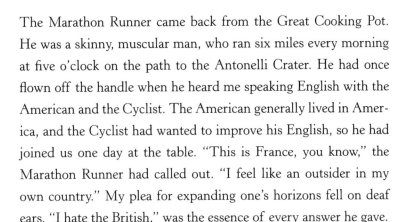

The Marathon Runner came back from the Great Cooking Pot. He was a skinny, muscular man, who ran six miles every morning at five o'clock on the path to the Antonelli Crater. He had once flown off the handle when he heard me speaking English with the American and the Cyclist. The American generally lived in America, and the Cyclist had wanted to improve his English, so he had joined us one day at the table. "This is France, you know," the Marathon Runner had called out. "I feel like an outsider in my own country." My plea for expanding one's horizons fell on deaf ears. "I hate the British," was the essence of every answer he gave.

The Marathon Runner claimed we'd make it back from Mount Fernand just before dark, and then we would meet up with the two biologists and return to the capital together.

We walked across garish green and dark red mosses; there was no path leading from the Great Plateau to Mount Fernand. The steamy ground was uneven. We made our way through jumbles of pebbles, boulders, and craters. Clover, club moss, and plantain grew among the rocks. We avoided the ferns, which often indicated one of the ubiquitous invisible holes. After reaching the Moorland Plateau, we crossed an overgrown ravine. With some effort I managed to pull myself up on the other side.

Mount Fernand looked like an unyielding, timeless wall. I was enveloped in the swirls of mist that the mountain was unable to shake off and that drove away all color. Although we wouldn't be able to see it ourselves, we knew that Mount Fernand plunged over two thousand feet straight into the sea, where it was flanked by the Balcony and the Railing. That was where the schooner had gone down for which the mountain had been named. The ship had slammed into the rocks during a violent gale, and fifteen crew members drowned. Only the captain and one of the sailors managed to pull themselves up onto the rocks. They survived on albatross eggs and fish until they were rescued by a passing Italian ship thirty-two days later.

The Marathon Runner was the first to enter the canebrake, while I followed at a great distance. The rushes were man-sized, and there was little space between them. They were rigid and had sharp points; everyone knew the story of the biologist who had lost an eye when he had fallen on one of the canes.

I felt my quadriceps swelling up; I could barely muster enough energy to raise my knee as I stepped. To clear a path I had to push aside the stalks, which was difficult to do in my stiff and very much oversized plastic waders. The stalks would often give way too easily, causing me to lose my balance and fall. The more I struggled, the harder it was for me to get back on my feet with my full rucksack. Occasionally I would just lie there, facedown, with my eyes closed, surrounded by crushed rushes.

At our last communication, the Marathon Runner had called over that we had another half an hour left. An hour and a half later I was on the verge of giving up, and had to summon all my willpower. I was still following the wall of mountain. When I reached the northwest slope, which seemed to be the least steep, I found the Marathon Runner waiting for me.

"Where's the path?" I asked.

"There isn't one. Just keep going up. If you lose your footing, grab on to the beach grass."

With my remaining strength I began the climb, but halfway up I turned around and let myself fall flat on my back. I couldn't think about anything else. "I'll just wait here," I said, and closed my eyes.

I was awakened by the cries of some yellow-nosed and sooty albatrosses, which had colonies high on the rocks and would circle the mountain in hundred-bird flocks. Though I knew better, I thought I could make out a mountainous archipelago in the blanket of clouds hanging over the ocean. The Marathon Runner appeared again an hour after he left. It was hard, he said, and he hadn't seen anything. "Not a thing—it was all hidden in the mist."

Amsterdam weather forecasts were seldom accurate, which was somewhat surprising in a place where every fifth person was a meteorologist and the streets were packed with rain gauges and sun photometers. Bonbon had explained to me that this was because the observations he and his colleagues made on Amsterdam were fed into a megacomputer in Toulouse, which integrated them into a global weather forecast they never got to see.

Amsterdam itself had been relegated to the extreme bottom corner of the regional weather map that hung in the meteorologists' office between two pairs of silicone breasts. The map consisted almost entirely of sea.

In order to attract as much attention as possible to their specialty, which seemed to be recording yesterday's weather, the meteorologists distributed a monthly overview full of columns showing the minimum and maximum temperatures, the amount of precipitation, and the number of days with fog. This data was cross-listed against the averages and records in each category.

The main problem facing the meteorologists was the wind. Amsterdam was situated in the emptiness of the southernmost part of the Southern Hemisphere, the cradle of never-ending storms that ran unchecked by any land. At times the wind had been so strong, it had blown away the anemometer. The wind tables were full of question marks: When I arrived, the instrument had been broken for six months. Paris kept on making promises, but the requested replacement parts still hadn't arrived.

The weather station was named after François Antonelli, a meteorologist who had fallen to his death from the tower in an attempt to repair the indicator on the anemometer. "He's buried on the island," Clammy told me, "but nobody remembers where the grave is."

The white, mosquelike station with its onion-shaped dome dominated the view of Amsterdam. From his drafting table in Paris, some architect had thought that a paved, rectilinear road with concrete blocks and square floodlights on either side would make just the right surroundings for the highest building on the island. The floodlights hadn't worked in years, and on an island without vehicular traffic, the access road looked like an empty highway in some small town in North Korea. Every weather station in the world releases a noontime sounding balloon, and Amsterdam was no exception; this was the only moment in the day when the stillness of the access road to the weather station was broken.

All ships traversing the Indian Ocean have the right to request data from the Amsterdam meteorological service, Bonbon told me. "At least the French ships do. But the basic policy is no weather forecasts for foreign ships."

Amsterdam is an island of gusty winds, aggressive fur seals, steep ravines, treacherous marshes, and falling rocks. Over the years, a number of meteorologists and biologists have lost their lives on the island; their names are listed on the monument to the dead. In light of the abundant danger, the district chief had decreed that no fewer than three men could embark on any potentially hazardous expedition or excursion.

The island was small, but inhospitable. The ground was pock-marked with hidden overgrown holes that could sprain your ankle. A few footpaths had been worn down here and there, but in many cases you had to make your own way over slopes ragged with bru-tally sharp rushes. You couldn't walk all the way around the island, since some areas were completely inaccessible: the Pearl Cliffs, the Great Slope of the Rushes, and the False Cape.

On the semiofficial topographical map, Amsterdam looked like an elliptical diamond with two blue spots—Salt Lake and Blue Lake—wedged between the Great Cooking Pot and Mount Dives, which peaked at nearly three thousand feet above sea level. Many of the islands' banks were steep, unapproachable cliffs that plunged straight into the sea.

Some of the names on the map were literal descriptions of the features themselves: Great Tunnel, Seal Bank, Red Grounds. The Foothills of the Rain Clouds and the Ravine of the Sleepwalkers had a certain dreamy quality. But many place-names smacked of compassion; it was part of a cartography of failures. A weather station, a cabin, a crater, and a small forest had all been named after Antonelli, who had fallen from the wind tower, while a cabin, a beach, and an anchorage all bore the name of the drowned sailor Ribault. Early disappointments were inscribed in the names False Cape and False Hébert Crater; the hubris implied by naming the second-highest summit Mount Olympus received its comeuppance in the fact that everyone simply called it "the False Peak."

The official names were designated by a committee in Paris. Similar committees had occasionally changed names for the other districts of the Southern Lands, if they deemed these unacceptable: Bismarck, Kaiser, and Kronprinz just wouldn't do for French islands, no matter how far away they might be. On Amsterdam, this wasn't necessary. Only one name had been scrapped, possibly from fear of provoking the Almighty: The Explosive Crater was now called the Great Cooking Pot.

Just like the paths that had spontaneously appeared around the island, certain rocks, ravines, peaks, and small lakes beyond the committee's purview had also acquired names that were passed down from one generation of residents to the next, and which reflected some of their deepest desires: Cape Bénédicte, Chantal Cave, the Virgin, and the Two Tits.

. . .

I came to know the feel of soft mosses underfoot; I learned to recognize which ferns might mask a lurking hole; I stretched my ankle muscles on the sloping hillsides. Amsterdam was always treacherous and unpredictable. You would struggle through two hours' worth of mud and then find the crater you had been hiking to had vanished—only to pop up again much farther away than when you started. Some peaks remained invisible from practically every angle, like Mount Dives, the island's highest point. There were also sheer cliffs and unexpected marshes that swallowed your leg and refused to let go.

But Amsterdam was also the island of the little rainbows. Although the skies were almost always gray and foggy, and the gusty air dripping with moisture, when the sun did make a brief appearance, the ocean vistas could be extraordinarily clear. North winds carried lukewarm air from the equator, which meant lingering rain and dense fog; south winds meant a drop in temperature and downpours or a chance of hail. The island was often agitated and nervous, but there were times when it rested and found a sort of peace that might last for days on end, whether beneath a dazzling sun or enshrouded in a cottony blanket of mist and fog.

Now that I had conquered the Great Plateau, I wanted to stand on top of Mount Dives as soon as possible. I didn't have to wait long. Three days after my first trek I was able to sign up for an expedition to the summit.

The day before our departure, the weather was downright summery: clear light, smooth seas, and a sultry breeze. The distant clouds looked like watercolors lightly brushed across an empty sky. The capital itself was cloudless; even the mists around the False Peak had parted, at least for a while. Despite all this, the Cyclist had predicted force eight winds for the following day, with powerful gusts and torrential rains in the highlands. This was by no means an uncommon local forecast; still, I had hoped our climb might be postponed a day, on the off-chance the weather might turn fair again—but alas: "The trip's still on. It'll be nice and bracing," said the American. "The forecast doesn't mean much, really. After all, wind and rain are *always* on the way out here." The American had a certain charismatic charm. He didn't give a damn about anybody or anything; all he cared about was trying to outdo himself. A professional mountain climber and glider pilot, he took part in as many expeditions as possible—the more difficult the better. He'd once had a near-fatal glider accident; his body still showed the scars, and he was missing half his ring finger.

We set out at five thirty in the morning. Even in January, it was cold. Amsterdam seemed incapable of absorbing any warmth: The island was just too small and the ocean too big. Louis and the Ascetic were on their way to d'Entrecasteaux with one of the aerometrics specialists; they still had at least nine hours to go. The American, David, and I would follow them to the foot of Mount Dives. David, another of the aerometrics specialists, wanted to see as much of the island as he could in as little time as possible, and didn't want to miss this opportunity. He'd intended to stay for a year and a half, but a few weeks after he arrived he learned that his girlfriend was—unexpectedly—pregnant; it must have happened on their last night together. David had asked permission to return to Paris on the *Marion Dufresne* when it next visited the island. His girlfriend was Jewish, just like his father. "Pure chance," David had said. "We met at a student demonstration."

After raiding the refrigerators in the kitchen, we set out from the capital, heading south. As soon as we passed the Malagasy Gardens, we left the path and started climbing the lower hills, which were covered in scarlet pimpernel and white clover. We followed an arbitrary route over the rocky grassland. "Your best landmark is that space between Lower Venus and Cyclops," the Ascetic told me, before he vanished from sight.

Over the next hour I caught an occasional glimpse of the phylica wood lower down; after that, the clouds rolled in and it started to pour. We continued our climb in waders and raincoats; it was tough going, but we closed our eyes and trudged ahead, soaking wet. Twice I stepped in a hole and lost my balance. When I reached the cowline I found the others waiting for me. We stepped over the barbed wire. After that we followed a worn-down, muddy trail into the eternal clouds of the interior highland. The False Peak and the Ship of Fire couldn't be far away, but all I could see were shadows. I suddenly realized how the Ascetic had once gotten lost in the fog. The ground was seldom even; the constant grade served as a reminder of the island's basic structure: an extinct, pointed volcano, with slopes scored by lava trenches and riddled with secondary craters.

On an island without roads or any means of transportation it was normal to walk a few hours every day. As a result, I was in much better shape than when I had arrived; my feet had grown accustomed to the sharp pieces of lava, the pebbles, and the gravel. I learned to pace myself while climbing, and not to allow myself to be rushed by men like the Ascetic, who had been clambering around Amsterdam for nearly a year and a half and who never seemed to feel anything that remotely resembled fatigue.

The wind started to pick up. A biologist on the *Marion Dufresne* had told me how he'd frequently been blown over during his expeditions in the high mountains of Amsterdam. "When the wind really gets going, your cheeks start to vibrate; I got the feeling they might be blown off at any moment." A short distance past the Tench's Mouth we reached the trail that led around the caldera. We pushed on through the mist; the clouds only opened sporadically to give us a glimpse of the ink-black Great March and the tiny blue-green lakes that dotted the primordial landscape.

It was blowing harder and harder. Now and then I felt as though I were walking into a wall, and when the gusts stopped, I lost my balance. While climbing the slopes I had kept myself going with the thought that the ground would soon level out and the climbing would be over. That turned out to be an illusion. The edge of the caldera turned out to a false plateau; the path kept going up and up. Then it led us around a mammoth wall of rock and all of a sudden we were sheltered from the ruthless wind.

Two hundred yards on, and two hours into the expedition, we took our first rest. The air was humid, but it wasn't raining. Without bothering to wipe off the mud, I plopped down on the ground. We ate thawed baguettes and peeled an orange; the Ascetic and Louis had a smoke, then they and the aerometrics specialist taped their boots shut for the trek through the great marsh that still lay ahead of them.

Following our break David, the American, and I began the final leg of our route: the climb up Mount Dives. Clammy had told me that some people chose to turn back at the foot of Mount Dives, since they were afraid of being overwhelmed by the surrounding endlessness, but that was exactly what I had been craving.

After a ten-minute climb, a small pile of stones indicated that we had reached the top. That should have been the crowning moment of all those years, of all my labors just to stand there on the top of the loneliest island on Earth and look around at the surrounding nothingness. But to my great disappointment I couldn't even see my own hand: The island's great height, combined with its isolated location, meant that clouds were constantly collecting around

Mount Dives and the High Plateau, even when the ocean was basking in bright sunshine a few hundred meters away. But the American remained optimistic.

We waited ten minutes, twenty, half an hour. . . . On the south side of the bare peak the wind was terrifically strong, so we lay down on the ground. After forty-five minutes we were chilled to the bone, so we gave up and started our descent. We'd been walking along the caldera for some time when the American called out, "Look! There's a break in the clouds. I don't know about you, but I'm going back up!"

With my last ounce of strength I dragged myself back uphill; I couldn't give up. When I once again reached the summit, there still wasn't much to see; the wind was driving the clouds at a relentless pace. But suddenly it was as if a circular curtain opened up. "A three-sixty!" yelled the American. And in a flash I saw the gray-green ocean far below, the edges of the island, massive Mount Fernand, the steel-blue pools in the caldera, the raised bumps, and jagged rubble all around. Far off, yellow-nosed albatrosses circled the Cathedral. Two great skuas dived into the depths of the crater, which was crisscrossed by deep trenches, while the trails of mist raced along the walls at great speed.

I lay flat on my stomach and peered into the abyss. This was a bleak landscape, still marked by violent upheaval, but one that offered the unforgettable sensation of seeing something completely untouched, a virginity preserved since prehistoric times.

I stood up and stepped away from David and the American. Against the vastness of the ocean, the island suddenly seemed much smaller: clearly laid out, yet vulnerable. For the first time in a long while I felt happy. I had made it to the top of Mount Dives, and was standing face-to-face with the infinity surrounding me. This was what I wanted: This was my life. It was as if I had regained control of my existence for a single, fleeting moment.

Fifteen minutes later the clouds came back, and the wind picked up again. We carefully made our way back down, toward the edge of the caldera. And once again it started pouring.

The true inhabitants of Martin-de-Viviès were the fur seals;
humans formed only an insignificant minority. Castaways had
long ago observed that each new phase of the moon could set off a
small tidal flood that overran the jetty, forcing the seals to seek
refuge on the higher rocks. In prolonged instances of high water
they would even invade the barracks and sheds of the capital. At
the time of our arrival, mating season had just begun, and my
room was permeated with the musky odor of the rutting males.
Hours later, even the rocks they had been basking on still reeked of
horny fur seal.

From a distance, their colonies sounded like outdoor swimming
pools on a summer day, filled with children's voices. At the same
time they provided a feast for the blue blowflies, and above all for
the wildcats. The latter kept hidden most of the time, but they
couldn't resist the lure of the placentas that suddenly appeared in
the tens of thousands.

Fur seals look like common seals but are larger and have external ears. They live in groups; they are strong and untamed. On

Amsterdam they clustered along the road to the jetty and dominated the high banks around the capital.

Their continued presence on the island was somewhat of a miracle. Ever since the arrival of the first humans, when De Vlamingh and his men had to kill "a host" of them that were "in the way," their lives had been under constant threat. The softness, warmth, and beauty of their fur kept their pelts in great demand until well into the nineteenth century. Europeans preferred the fur of the males, which they used to wrap their harnesses, and line their shoes and boots. The fur of the females fetched a high price in China, where it was made into garments and linings. Starving hunters and castaways had also tried eating the seals, but except for the newborn pups, the meat was tough.

The key to a successful hunt was surprise, which the hunters achieved by stalking their prey against the wind, hunched over, each man following in the footsteps of his predecessor. A sharp blow between the eyes with a club or mallet put the first seal out of commission. After that, the idea was to block the path of as many seals as possible and beat them down before the whole colony fled to the sea in panic. Killing a female had an extra advantage: Because the young instinctively returned to their mothers, the hunters would likely be able to skin one or more pups after their initial kill.

With near-surgical precision, the trappers would slit open the dead animals along the ventral side—starting at the chin, moving past the throat, and continuing on down to the tail. Then they cut away the limbs from the inside and carefully stripped away the skin. At the end of the day they scraped the meat from the pelts and removed the inches-thick layer of fat underneath. Then the pelts were salted, shined up, folded, and stacked into piles. Great skuas and albatrosses flocked to feast on the blood and entrails, so that by the next morning the beach was clean.

After over a hundred years of organized destruction, the seals of Amsterdam had nearly become extinct. Probably less than a hundred adult individuals managed to survive the ongoing mass slaughter—by hiding in more secluded colonies at Wolf Fish Inlet and Boulder Coast, which were inaccessible to humans.

It was only after the construction of the capital that the seals were left in peace. They began reclaiming territory—at first, hesitantly, but as time went on they became increasingly bold. Soon they had started new colonies on every shore they could swim to, as the old settlements became more and more densely populated. The steady growth brought an unprecedented population explosion, so that the seals soon numbered in the tens of thousands. They hadn't mixed with any other species; these fur seals were the direct descendants of the hundred who had survived the trappers' reign of terror. Never again would they let themselves be driven off.

Fur seal pups could be found in practically every shoreside nook and cranny. They hid behind the rocks and bleated like sheep. Louis and the Ascetic were skilled at boxing them in and grabbing hold of them. They weighed the pups and, using a special stapler, attached a plastic identification tab to their hind flippers. They also collected fresh seal droppings, which they would clean of mud, straw, and dead insects during the winter months before shipping the samples to Paris. There, the seals' diet would be analyzed in a lab.

. . .

While the entire population was never on the island at any given moment, the colonies were most densely populated during mating season. Approaching an adult was always a dangerous undertaking: Perhaps they remembered that humans were not to be trusted. While some of them merely raised an eyelid, others growled and bared their teeth, sending threads of thick, warm spit dribbling down against their chins. The most aggressive seals would even give chase. Their jaws could easily bite off your arm.

Although preservation of the species took place entirely on shore, fur seals have always been creatures of the sea. All their activities on land seem painful: dragging themselves over the sharp rocks; the struggle for hegemony within the colony; and even the act of mating, which looked quite a lot like a brutal rape. One morning I saw two pups sleeping on the decomposing body of a half-grown male. Was it their older brother, their cousin, or just a comfortable place to rest their heads?

A day before they deliver their pups, the females return to the island. The mothers and children had one week to learn to recognize each other's voice and scent; this would later be indispensable for finding each other in the midst of thousands of other seals. During that same period the females were covered again. "They're pregnant their whole lives," Louis had told me. "The new embryo is carried by the females for months, as a sort of extra supply. It won't start to grow until later."

Skipping from one rock to the next, I explored the colony behind the monument to the dead. It reeked of fish and of decay. Some of the young had just lost their mother, and were near starvation or had just succumbed.

In fur seal society, individual relations are always on a razor's edge: Apart from one week a year, the females are continuously pregnant, while a great many males would never manage to mate. The struggle is simple, but ruthless. Every year the males are the first to come ashore. Vicious one-on-one duels determine the hierarchy of the colony. The strongest get the best positions: up front, but beyond the reach of the waves; the majority are banished to the periphery. As a reward for their invincibility, the highest-ranking males are allowed to fertilize as many females as they can. It's as if they sense this might be their only chance to mate, and in most cases, it was. Some of them might drag twenty females by the scruff of the neck to the Elephant Pool in a single season.

Females have no say in their subjugation. Perhaps they have resigned themselves to their fate, in the knowledge that only a small group of males will cover them each year, so that mainly they are the ones who pass on the genes of the species. The females are also spared the long, difficult journey to the surf: they always mate, calve, and nurse their young inside the main colony, lying in groups close to their impregnator—inasmuch as he can be found, since the bulls are constantly getting into scuffles. They are utterly focused on protecting their territory, and always ready to conquer and mate.

The males who have been driven away from the coastal strip are forced to flee inland, full of bites and bloody wounds. These "second class" seals have their fights, too. The weakest, most cowardly, or most peace-loving seals are ultimately banished to the rocks near the lava strip, where they lie stretched out on the ground, most of them wounded. The bull seals go all out, sometimes fighting to the death. Once in the water they are free, but every year they are destined to return to land, where the frustrated males are permanently relegated to the loser's beach.

I continued my search for absolute and utter solitude. Because of safety regulations there was only one place where I was permitted to spend the night away from the company of others, where I might escape the oppressive atmosphere of the capital: the Antonelli cabin. The district chief told me I could stay there for three days, as long as I took a walkie-talkie and checked in with the communication center twice a day.

The cabin was a forty-five-minute walk from the capital. In my rucksack I had four bottles of water, a couple onions, a piece of cheese, some tomatoes, two steaks, my last three bottles of wine, and a few books. In addition, the shelter was always stocked with emergency supplies. I borrowed a sleeping bag from the American and packed my own pillow.

The Antonelli cabin was located at the edge of the crater of the same name, southwest of the capital. This was by no means a true trek; the route was perhaps the easiest on the whole island: a broad gravel path ran from the Malagasy Gardens practically up to the cabin porch.

On the town square I said hello first to the Marathon Runner and then to the Slaughterer, who was on his knees, planting seeds. As I made my way out of the capital I heard a faint shout and the sound of a power drill. Then these sounds, too, faded away, as the path snaked around craters and rocks, over an undulating, well-grazed landscape. In the distance I saw the silhouette of a bull, massive and motionless, but the minute he noticed my presence he backed off, slowly and cautiously.

The sky was cloudy, but there was almost no wind, and the air was dry. From the path I had an unbroken view of the ocean. I could see the Lone Tree—a single phylica from long ago that had survived all the fires and trappers and aurochs. In admiration for its tenacity, the tree had been fenced off with barbed wire, to protect it from the cows.

After a half hour's walk, a small white patch appeared on the horizon: the site of my self-imposed three-day exile. I left the path and scrambled across the damp meadows, through the ferns and yellow-and-white marguerites. Fresh cow patties were swarming with blowflies. The last leg of the hike was an almost perpendicular climb up to the edge of the crater, beyond which was a small wood that was sheltered from the winds, somber and sedate. The cabin itself was perched on the very edge of the crater. A crumbling wooden porch overlooked the forest and the sea; the district chief had warned me not to trust the balustrade.

Though the Antonelli cabin might count as one of the world's most isolated hermitages, the facilities were more than adequate: I had a cooking stove and a supply of ready-made canned dinners, which were past date but not too rusty. There were four chairs around the dinner table, and two gas lanterns.

My first order of business was to sweep up the myriad dead

blowflies and beat the dust out of the mattress on the bottom bunk. I heard a rustling in the corner; evidently I'd be sharing the cabin with a mouse or two. Outside I found a grill set up beneath an overhang, but I had no intention of using it: I make it a general rule to avoid confrontations with mechanical appliances.

I pulled out a chair and poured myself a glass of Beaujolais. The sea appeared calm; the air smelled of damp wood. I gazed out at the colorless hillsides of the island I had begun to love. This was the ultimate frontier; I could go no farther. I was truly at the periphery of the world, thousands of miles away from the nearest land.

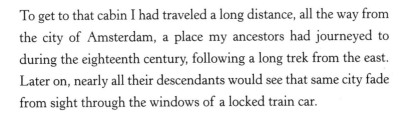

To get to that cabin I had traveled a long distance, all the way from the city of Amsterdam, a place my ancestors had journeyed to during the eighteenth century, following a long trek from the east. Later on, nearly all their descendants would see that same city fade from sight through the windows of a locked train car.

They had come to the Netherlands from Germany, and settled outside Amsterdam in one of the rural Jewish communities known as the *mediene*. My forefather Elias Salomon, gravedigger by trade, left there and settled by "the Toll Bridge on the Amstel," just outside the city limits. Eventually his children moved into the city itself, to Weesperstreet and Rapenburg quarter. Jacob Elias, the eldest son of the gravedigger, opened a butcher's shop on Jodenbreestraat (literally: the Jews' Broad Street), which was taken over after his death by his son Elias, who moved it to the Leper's canal.

His son Jacob, my great-grandfather, started a wholesale business in kosher cheese. With the help of a new rind-making technique, he became the first person to be able to export Dutch cheese to other countries—a far cry from the days when his ancestors, barred from settling anywhere permanently, peddled oranges and lemons from one eastern Dutch village to the next. By Jacob's time, the languages they had once brought with them had disappeared; even the marriage certificates were no longer signed with Hebrew characters.

Jacob's warehouses were in the heart of the old Jewish quarter, but he himself soon moved to Weesperzijde Road, to a house that overlooked the river, a few miles upstream from where his great-grandfather had buried the dead. My grandfather Samuel followed his father in the cheese trade.

Years after my father's death, I met an elderly woman at a birthday party who told me that, through her curtains, she had witnessed the moment when Samuel and his wife Elisabeth had left the city once and for all. "Blankets," the woman said. "Your grandparents both had blankets under their arms. That's what I saw when they were taken from their home." In silence, they had joined their neighbors in the group being rounded up by policemen in black uniforms. The following day they left Amsterdam, to the rhythm of the rails, traveling east, the same direction from where their ancestors once had come.

A few months earlier, my father, along with two hundred other boys like him, had been brought to the courtyard of a school not far from his parents' house. There they were made to stand in formation. My father found himself next to an older man, who, glancing at the exit, whispered for my father not to make a move. As soon as the guards began taking the detainees inside, the man signaled to my father, and they ran off together in the twilight. No one chased after them. My father went into hiding. Later that week he went home one last time. My grandfather wasn't there. My grandmother gave him her diamond broach, which she always wore on festive occasions, and a picture of herself. That day my father was wearing a pair of rust-brown knickers and a blue tie. The same tie survived years of hiding in darkened attic rooms; my father kept it for years, until the day he accidentally threw it away.

I never asked my father very many questions. He dealt in ladies' textiles of the cheapest sort, but he had a sense of humor about the quality of his wares: "Three washes and there's nothing left but buttons," he once told me. I often went with him to soccer matches. He had a regular seat in the middle of a bunch of cigar-smoking men who wore beige raincoats and checkered caps on their balding heads: in other words, men just like him. The way he saw it, he had been playing in "overtime" for much of his life: "I really shouldn't even be here."

His last wish was for a view of the sea; we buried him on the highest dune of a cemetery on the coast.

I poured myself another glass of wine. A gentle rain had begun to fall, but the porch had a roof, and since there wasn't any wind, I didn't feel cold. I thought of the many nights I had spent entering the names of seven generations of ancestors into my computer. I thought about my unrelenting attempts to control my life by trying to put everything in order.

The discovery had been a complete surprise. I had gone with my mother to the Auschwitz commemoration ceremony at Wertheim

Park, in part to honor the memory of my father's parents. I asked her which camp her family had been deported to. "Sobibor," she said. "Almost all my uncles and aunts died there."

Afterward we walked diagonally across the street to visit the Hollandsche Schouwburg. Now an "educational monument," the building had once been a theater; during the war it was turned into a collecting point where all those about to be deported spent their last night in Amsterdam. My mother paused in front of a glass display case with postcards. And then she froze. "That card was written by Uncle Bram and Aunt Liesje!" she cried out. It was an improvised postcard, which my mother's aunt and uncle must have thrown out of the train as it was pulling away. It was dated "train 9 o'clock" and, judging from the postmark, had been mailed by someone in Amersfoort.

"Dear Else, greetings from the train," Liesje had written to her daughter. "I'm sure you understand how we feel about everything, but what can we do? We know you've all done your best. Be brave, we'll try and do the same. Keep calm; no one can escape his fate. A thousand kisses, be sensible. Your loving M."

The only surviving picture of my grandparents had been taken at a party. With a bottle of champagne in a bucket of ice, they are ringing in the New Year—1939. My grandfather was fifty-two and my grandmother was forty-two when they died, having suc- cumbed to "the effects of disease, exhaustion or gassing at, or in the immediate vicinity of, Auschwitz, some time after August 10 but no later than August 31, 1942," according to the Red Cross.

My grandparents left virtually no tangible trace of their existence. But just the same, they would never again leave home and family—even though we never talked about their fate.

Elias Salomon of "the Toll Bridge on the Amstel" had scores of descendants, but of these only my father, his cousin Jack, and his cousin Frieda remained. Frieda never shared her life with men and remained childless. Jack had three sons who were Parisians and no longer knew how to pronounce their own last name. Two of them were gay and had no children; the third had a daughter and a son.

On one of my visits to Paris to pursue my case with the administration of the Southern Lands, I had looked up my second cousin Olaf. He showed me the grave of his Moroccan boyfriend Jamal. Twice a week Olaf sent his former lover a letter, which was placed on the tomb by the cemetery caretaker. The grave was in a family plot belonging to Olaf's mother; by a strange twist of fate it was also the final resting place of the brother of a convicted war criminal. My second cousin had had a marble memorial placed at the gravesite, with a white horse's head three-and-a-half yards tall. "That way it's considered a monument and won't be removed, even after fifty years. And you can see it from a distance," he said. A relative of the war criminal's brother had looked at the new addition in amazement and blurted out, "What's that Arab doing here all of a sudden?"

My second cousin visited the cemetery every week; he cleaned the marble with a cloth. "Even the rich have to die," someone had scrawled in felt-tipped marker on the ostentatious tomb. After that, Olaf had the base replaced with one made of black marble. Meanwhile he had had his own name inscribed next to his lover's; only the date needed to be filled in.

. . .

It was getting colder, so I went inside. All at once my eighty-year-old aunt flashed before my eyes. She had recently become addicted to a computer game in which you could shoot Germans, who shouted *"Dein Leben!"* or *"Stehen bleiben!"* My aunt knew no mercy. In the newer versions of the game the Germans were replaced by monsters, but my aunt would have none of that. My own reaction was different. As a child I never accepted any candy that came wrapped, because I never knew what to do with the paper afterward. At our house you didn't cry and you didn't throw things. You didn't yell or swear and you ate properly, with a knife and fork. "Except for chicken. You're allowed to eat chicken with your fingers," said my mother. "Although I wouldn't."

My second day at the cabin I climbed down the steep slope and made my way through the bushes to the bottom of the crater. The grove that had been planted thirty years before was still thriving, a living memorial to the man who had fallen from the wind tower. Along the edges were apple trees, pressed up against the mossy slopes of the crater; a dense clump of spruce trees filled the center of the circular wood. Up on the porch a stiff breeze had started to blow, but in the dark shelter of the crater, the spruce branches hung there, motionless. I walked all around the grove, then, clinging to the shrubs for support, I pulled myself back up the slope and headed toward the cabin.

I didn't touch the canned food; I just fried a steak and wolfed it down with a baguette and a piece of cheese. Later, as the clouds turned orange and the hills went black, I jerked off among the rushes. I'd never been so absolutely certain that no one could see me.

My stay at the cabin came to an end; the last morning was bright and sunny. I thought about the scorching hot days back in the city of Amsterdam, when I had forced myself to stay inside, moody and impatient for the night—despite the fact that I loved the warmth. And even though I was now utterly alone on a corner of the most remote island on earth, I no longer felt that same sense of loneliness. Here I felt fully connected to the life around me: rocks and wind, albatrosses and seals, biologists and meteorologists.

They said that it was because of the storms: The strong winds gave people high blood pressure; some became short-tempered, others depressed. I had checked out a report from the library in the Great Skua, in which a former district chief described his experiences with the Blue Monk, possibly the loneliest resident in the history of Amsterdam. The man had been posted to the island as a meteorologist, in a mission that included the Sergeant, the Canadian, the Uncle, and the Fat Alsatian—all coarse men who used coarse language. It wasn't long after Antonelli's fatal fall. The meteorologists who came after him refused to have anything to do with wind towers; they left a newly delivered structure in the garage.

The Blue Monk was still just a boy. He always wore blue overalls and often withdrew from the others just to stare at the sea for hours on end. The district chief found him to be on edge—nervous and unsociable.

The Monk was constantly at odds with his colleagues. Within a few weeks he began neglecting his duties; he was rarely on time, and was careless with his instruments, which he would simply leave lying around. Increasingly, he became the cause of insinua-

tions and arguments. At the same time he refused to conduct any
more meteorological observations or work the early shift. One
morning, without the slightest provocation, he picked up a ham-
mer and started swinging it around until he broke a calibrated
barometer. Afterward he just laughed and asked for a cigarette.
Eventually he resumed his duties, but he kept to himself more and
more. The district chief asked him to shave his beard so it
wouldn't hide his face, but the Blue Monk refused.

The boy often visited the rocks near the monument to the dead.
He was quiet and tended to daydream during mealtimes. One day
he disappeared. The gardener had been the last to see him, wandering around the basalt flats on the eastern coast, so they went to
look, but to no avail. Then, two days later, the Monk returned,
wearing his overalls. All he said was that he had wanted to be
alone. That evening he came to dinner, but disappeared again
halfway through the meal.

While the others were eating their lobster they suddenly heard a
loud bang coming from the west. With the district chief in the
lead, they ran in the direction of the noise. They found him on the
trash heap:

*There, by the cliff where we dumped our garbage, below the
monument where a few cheerless nasturtiums wither beneath the
gilded letters, where the cow manure drips off the mountain ridge
onto the jumble of rotting guts and cattle carcasses, empty barrels and scraps of wood.*

*There lay the child in blue. The explosives had ripped open his
intestines. The car battery had come undone, and acid was flow-
ing down his sides. The copper wire gently brushed against his*

nose. His riddled face was white, his eyes wide-open. He had carefully prepared everything: the yellow wire around his belly, the detonating mechanism that ran from his belt to the battery and to the explosives.

They carefully carried the Blue Monk back to the settlement and laid him out on the Ping-Pong table. Later they buried him by Dumas Crater. The district chief did not believe the Blue Monk had any illness. "So he was free. He chose death by his own hand over life in a collective that was devoid of human warmth."

At the end of that same day I returned to the capital, but instead of taking the path, I decided to cut straight through the hills, which were dotted with orange hawkweed. I stopped at the Lone Tree and, using the automatic timer, snapped a picture of the two of us. Before long I could see the dome of the weather station, still a ways off; the shoreline was littered with numerous antennas that had been blown down or snapped off by the wind.

At the end of the boulevard Martin-de-Viviès, I saw Annabelle, a newborn calf that had been brought back the previous year by the hunter who had shot her mother. Keeping cats or dogs as pets was not allowed, so Annabelle immediately became the center of attention. The men of Mission 48 showered her with affection, feeding her with the bottle and petting her.

Although she came from a wild herd, Annabelle seemed fully reconciled to her new, domesticated life. She roamed the streets and grazed among the cypresses and the alders of AmsParc. She nibbled the flowers in the flowerbeds and deposited her patties by the barracks, out of the wind. Still, she was pretty big, with a nice pair of horns, and in recent weeks she had grown increasingly feisty. So I decided to avoid her, and returned to my room by a roundabout route, past the Great Skua and the laundry room—ignoring the advice I had received from Clammy: "You've got to grab an animal like that by the nose and give it a good, hard twist. That's how we do it in the mountains."

In fact, the very next day, Annabelle almost gored both Kaplan and the Greek, so the district chief decided to intervene at once. He ordered that the animal be slaughtered that same day. This was within the authority of any number of his capacities—as mayor, as chief of police, and as gamekeeper. But others, especially the Dreamer, were very much opposed. Some of the dissenters felt they should at least try to release Annabelle on the other side of the cowline, in the hope she might be accepted into one of the roaming herds of aurochs. But the biologists were skeptical; they believed the animal would die of hunger and thirst, as she was used to being served bowls of fresh drinking water, and unaccustomed to licking off the morning dew. In the end, the chief relented. He ordered Annabelle placed in a trailer and taken to the foot of the Antonelli; after that her fate would be in the hands of the aurochs.

The animal seemed to sense her impending doom: Whenever anyone tried to approach her, she would take to her heels. Eventually they caught her with a lasso. Then, with two tractors at the ready and using an old hoist, the district chief and the Chimney succeeded in getting the calf on the trailer—except Annabelle managed to climb over the edge and jump out three different times.

The next day the ceremony was repeated. This time the Chimney had dipped into his stock of tranquilizers, and while the Dreamer looked on in disgust, he went at Annabelle with a big hypodermic, although even that failed to knock her out completely.

The next day she was back. The Marathon Runner was the first to see her, when he went out for his early morning run. Annabelle was standing in front of the post office. No one could explain how she'd been able to find her way, or how she had passed through the barbed wire. But there she was. The district chief decided to let the matter rest for the time being, since he had enough to do as it was.

The barrack known as the Residence was one of the few buildings on the island where the walls were free of pin-ups. Instead, there was a photograph of the French president above the chief's desk (there was also one in the post office). The chief himself was rarely in his office, though, since he generally preferred to spend his time exterminating rats or maintaining the capital's green spaces. No matter where he was, he tended to wear shorts and a T-shirt even. He had been personally appointed by the administrateur, who had his own room in the Residency reserved for his exclusive use, for the two days a year that he might choose to spend on the island.

The district chief seemed all-powerful. He could arrest people or banish them; he was head of the volunteer fire company, and next to his desk was a safe with weapons and ammunition. He was also in charge of the transmitting station, and on an island without regular telephone traffic, this meant he was in control of all outgoing messages. As chief customs officer he was also responsible for all incoming goods.

He showed me the civil register. No one had ever been born or married on Amsterdam, so the only record with any entries listed the names of the dead. When I started to leaf through it, he shut the book again: "That's confidential. It contains detailed descriptions of the deaths."

Just a few years earlier, the district chief had had a chance to assert his authority in a maritime issue of international proportions. The radiotelegraph operator had received an SOS from a Japanese ship, which reported that one of the tuna boats in its squadron had been shipwrecked on Saint-Paul. Because of the dense fog, the boat—which had been operating in violation of international law—had been navigating on automatic pilot. No one had been on the bridge; all twenty-two crew members were watching a video. They were taken completely by surprise when, without any warning, the ship struck the rocks. The men made it ashore uninjured, but the ship was lost.

The district chief took the emergency plan out of the cabinet. Step 1: Notify the administration of the Southern Lands. But everyone at headquarters in Paris was on vacation except for one woman on staff, who suggested the chief sail to Saint-Paul and raise the French flag "to show them that it's ours." The chief didn't have to ask whether such a display of patriotism was the most appropriate response, given the precarious situation in which the crew found itself. Amsterdam didn't even have a boat.

Meanwhile, a rainstorm had started up; the swells were so high that no ship could manage the approach to Saint-Paul. A few days later, an Australian Hercules transport plane took off from Mauritius to drop some supplies for the castaways. The pilot attempted to contact Amsterdam's communication center, but the radiotelegraph operator couldn't understand him. The man sprinted up to the geophysics laboratory as fast as he could to find someone who spoke English, but by then it was too late: The Hercules was already cruising over Mount Dives on its way to Saint-Paul, where the castaways wandered around aimlessly during the day and piled into the only cabin at night. The food was dropped from the plane with parachutes.

After ten days the wind died down, and a French ship managed to rescue the fishermen. They were examined at the hospital on Amsterdam and later picked up by a passing Japanese whaler. On the open sea, the captain of the stranded fishing boat was transferred to a French ship, which had set out from Réunion with a gendarme on board. The plan was to bring the captain to Amsterdam, where the district chief, in his role as public prosecutor, would interrogate him; that would make Paris sit up and take notice. But the wind was getting stronger, the swells were getting higher, and neither the Japanese captain nor the gendarme could make it ashore—not even with the so-called wet-landing method. The waves battered the rocks, and the man made it clear that he feared for his life. After two days they gave up, and the ship sailed off with the captive captain.

"That took us down a peg," said one of the aerometrics specialists who had been on Amsterdam during the shipwreck. "There they were, on an island surrounded by thousands of miles of open sea. Meanwhile we were fifty miles away and couldn't do a thing about it. We felt totally useless."

The wreck has never been recovered, but it was later examined by representatives of the Southern Lands: The logbook had vanished, and all they found was a trunkful of waterlogged porn films.

At the beginning of the third week in January, the Biosol planned to go to Cape Del Cano to count thistles: The time had finally come for me to see for myself whether Willem de Vlamingh had been able to land at the island's southernmost point.

On the day of our outing the air was misty and filled with ozone. We set off in the early morning twilight, accompanied by Kaplan. The Biosol figured that the hike to the "biologists' hotel" on Cape Del Cano would take seven hours. Cape Vlaming was on the way.

Because the cape was surrounded by steep ravines, it could not be reached from the plateau: The only way of getting there was to follow the shoreline from the northeastern part of the island to the southwest.

We started off on the route that led to the phylica forest. As soon as we left the path, the Biosol bounded out ahead of us with his long legs; twenty minutes later Kaplan, too, disappeared from view. There was a cold southern wind and a rainbow over Cyclops. I met up with the Biosol at the spot where one of his predecessors had fallen off the rock face. An iron memorial plaque bearing the man's name and the date of his death had been affixed to the cliff where he had taken his last step. He had gone there with a colleague to ring the terns on the beach. The one stood at the top, while the other lowered himself down on the rope. But halfway down he slammed into a rock and lost his grip.

I crawled on my belly to the edge of the precipice and looked down 150 feet, where the waves were hammering against the large, coal-black rocks. Afterward we resumed our journey, in silence. We waded through the water that was running off the mountain, and then descended into the Ravine of the Sleepwalkers, which was covered with dense vegetation. A tranquil waterfall emerged in the distance, a stripe of silver gleaming on the foggy slope.

Following Kaplan's footsteps, I passed the peak of the Kettle and Cape Novara, the easternmost point of the island. The Foothills of the Rain Clouds came vaguely into view; we could make out the silhouette of the summit, some 2,300 feet above sea level. We hiked up and down the gently rolling, mossy hills, with the double peak of the Two Tits in the background.

The rain started coming down hard; I put on my waders and the orange plastic raincoat. Near the False Hébert we were met by violent gusts of wind. Cape Vlaming couldn't be much farther away, but when I again caught up with the Biosol, he told me we wouldn't be able stop after all. "I have no idea exactly where Cape Vlaming is," he said. "No one ever goes there. We've got to get to Del Cano as soon as possible. Otherwise we'll be in trouble, at least if we keep going at this pace."

Through the pelting rain we walked for half an hour straight across a slanting slope. Below us, the sea was foaming and churning. To our left was the ravine; the Slope of the Rushes rose on our right—an inaccessible high bluff surrounded by fog. After seven hours on my feet, I finally managed to struggle up the last ravine. But then, as an added bonus, we had to push through a dense canebrake before we reached our lodging for the next two nights.

"The biologists' hotel," the Biosol said, and pointed to a wooden box.

I looked at him quizzically.

"I mean it, that's really it," he said. "In this weather it isn't feasible to try to pitch a tent."

There was no door; the box was simply open on one side. That meant the rain could come through, but the Biosol constructed a little wall using the plastic barrels containing ready-made dinners that were stored in the box. In view of the relentless squalls, he tied the barrels together with rope.

We crawled into the box, gobbled down some bread, and within fifteen minutes were sound asleep. The Biosol slept near the open side and woke up soaked the next morning.

That day the squalls continued, and the weather remained cloudy, misty, cold, and damp. The wind was so strong that the waves were blown back like fountains before they reached the cliffs. We climbed down to Cape Del Cano, which offered a breathtaking view of the bay. The greenish-brown cliffs were over two thousand feet high, and plunged into the waves at a nearly 90-degree angle. It was plain to see how in prehistoric times the rest of the island had broken off at this point and fallen into the depths of the ocean, forever lost. Farther off, we could see the Cathedral, like a guard defending Cape d'Entrecasteaux from the ferocious surf. Thousands of yellow-nosed albatrosses were circling above the high, craggy peak and along the misty slopes of the Great Balcony.

In the pouring rain Kaplan and I returned to the box, numb with cold. Meanwhile the Biosol had marked off an area of two thousand square feet, and had begun counting thistles. The tally was a contraindication of the state of the landscape: the fewer thistles, the more room for indigenous grasses and rushes. The destruction of the native vegetation—mostly from the peat fires—had been followed by an explosive growth of thistles, among other things.

The Biosol came from a farming family in the Alps. He was a loner and tended to keep to himself, even at parties. Now, too, he refused our offers to help to count the thistles. Today was his birthday, but he preferred to celebrate in a leaky box rather than at the bar of the Great Skua. Toward nightfall we downed the bottles of wine that we had brought along, and I learned that you can dry drenched clothes with your own body heat by stuffing them into the foot of your sleeping bag.

The third day we left as early as possible, in order to stop at Cape Vlaming. I had run out of clean clothes, and at breakfast we drank wine to stay warm. The wind had died down a bit, but the waves were bigger and the foam higher. "The sea is sluggish," said the Biosol.

The Hébert Crater was incorrectly marked on the map, and the False Hébert was entirely absent. That made it difficult to determine the location of Cape Vlaming. The Biosol walked at a fast pace. I was almost afraid that he'd keep on going until he reached the capital. "Are we there yet?" I asked.

"Cape Vlaming is nothing but a name," answered the Biosol. "Really, that's all it is, nothing."

"But where *is* that nothing? There's got to be something, some rock or ledge they gave the name to?"

The Biosol walked on without saying anything, and a short time later he pointed to the cliff: "Cape Vlaming."

I looked down, but quickly pulled back. A vertical wall; no one who landed there would have lived to tell about it.

"Of course it could have looked very different three hundred years ago," said the Biosol consolingly. "With every storm or hurricane, another chunk of rock or a pebble beach disappears into the sea somewhere or another."

He had turned his back to the shore and was taking pictures of the steep rockface. After that he took out another map, in order to determine our position, using the Foothills of the Rain Clouds, the half-collapsed Hébert, and the False Hébert as orientation points. "I made a mistake. It's another couple hundred yards farther along," he said.

The "new" Cape Vlaming was a triangular plateau, with sheer cliffs on the sides. It looked like a slice of pie that had been cut out with razor-sharp precision. For the second time I jubilantly posed for a photograph.

Where the cliffs ran into the water there were no boulders to break the impact of the waves as they burst against the cape, sending jets of water dozens of yards into the air. One thing was certain: Willem de Vlamingh never landed here. The only remaining possibility was Wolf Fish Inlet, a small, secluded beach near Cape d'Entrecasteaux, which the crew of the *Geelvinck* must have sighted as they approached the island.

Immediately upon returning to the capital we learned the sensational news that a fisherman from a nearby fishing trawler was on his way to our local hospital. Only one company, a French concern, had permission to fish for lobster in the territorial waters of Amsterdam and Saint-Paul, which they could do no more than twice a year. The fishermen were Creoles from Réunion, the officers Bretons. The captain of the ship currently trawling the area had reported that one of the fishermen was suffering from acute heart problems. Conveying him to the nearest city would take at least a week, and seemed too risky on a fishing boat pitching about on the waves without full medical facilities. After a consultation over a marine phone, the Chimney decided that the fisherman should be admitted to the hospital on Amsterdam right away. Since the patient was able to stand, the district chief opted for a "forklift landing."

The next morning the fishing boat showed up off the island, but the sea was too heavy to attempt the landing. After midnight the wind died down. Not wanting to waste any time, the district chief ordered a nighttime disembarkation. The fishing boat lit the ocean with a floodlight. The patient climbed down a rope ladder into an inflatable rubber raft; it was calmer on the open sea than by the cliffs. The Chimney and the district chief had donned helmets and oilskins and were pacing nervously back and forth. The only lighting on the pier came from a single measly streetlamp. In the distance, the fishing boat looked like an absurdly large and bare Christmas tree in the middle of a deserted shopping street.

Longhaired Nico drove up in the forklift, which he used to secure a steel ladder on the pier above the surging water. The fisherman stood up on unsteady legs in the small, rocking raft, ready to grab on to the rungs of the ladder.

"The swells are too high. This is insane," the district chief yelled over the noise of the tractors and the breakers. He decided to try a "wet landing" on losers' beach instead. This was a technique used only in dire emergencies, and it meant that the fisherman would get wet—which, in view of his condition, also entailed some risk.

The helmsman of the rubber boat waited until he thought the sea had calmed down at least for a moment. He brought the raft in close enough to the beach for the patient to jump onto the rocks, right among the frustrated fur seals. Then, while practically the entire population of Martin-de-Viviès looked on, the tractor hauled the patient to the hospital in a trailer.

The island hospital had an operating theater, a radiology room, a dentist's chair, and a small ward. Boots and climbing shoes were kept in the entrance hall; inside, you had to walk around in stocking feet or slippers. The ashcan was invariably full to the point of overflowing, mostly with the Chimney's own cigarette butts. He was a military doctor, fresh out of medical school; before being dispatched to the island he had taken special courses in surgery, anesthesiology, dentistry, psychopathology, and biology.

On Amsterdam there was no flu; a few times a year the *Marion Dufresne* might bring some viruses, but there were too few potential hosts for these to survive. The Chimney's chief job consisted of treating wounds and oral infections. One of his predecessors had performed an appendectomy that lasted two hours, and a colleague in the similar hospital on the Kerguelen Islands had had to amputate the leg of an injured Ukrainian fisherman. Meteorologists, volcanologists, and handymen functioned as instant nurses or assistant anesthetists to help assist with the operations.

The Chimney had recently started presenting the first part of the mandatory first aid course, although up to that point most of us hadn't bothered to attend. He now scrambled together two teams of nurses, and via Inmarsat connection, consulted with a cardiologist in a suburb of Marseille. He then decided to place the fisherman in intensive care indefinitely.

Two days later I was on duty. The fisherman was asleep; his condition was stable, and his life was not in danger. My training as head cardiologic nurse had lasted exactly five minutes. I had been told to observe the patient regularly and help him wash himself or go to the toilet. If one of the lights started to blink I was supposed to turn the yellow knob, but if the machine started beeping I was simply to ignore it. "Just press 'SILENCE,'" the Chimney had said. If the patient's systolic pressure fell below one hundred or the pulse went below forty, I was to wake the Chimney immediately. He slept above the ward.

Every hour I read the patient's blood pressure and pulse from the monitors at his bedside and noted them on one of the military hospital forms from the stack in the Chimney's office. Name. Rank. Corps. Ward. Bed. Class. The patient's charts were forwarded to the senior medical officer's desk—amid the piles of comic books, packs of chewing gum, and medical handbooks. It smelled of disinfectant.

Every time the fisherman woke up, he thanked me profusely for my concern. I told him it wasn't necessary, "You're our guest. On Amsterdam, everybody is equal."

The heart patient was soon pronounced out of danger. The lobster boat had stayed in the area and returned after a few days to pick him up and drop him off as soon as possible at the nearest hospital, nearly two thousand miles away.

The boat where the patient worked was a floating fish factory, where the lobsters that were caught were immediately frozen. All previous attempts at processing the fish on the islands themselves had ended in catastrophic failure.

Some time after the French had taken definitive possession of Amsterdam and Saint-Paul, a Breton ship owner was granted a concession to exploit the two islands for a period of thirty-five years. In the late 1920s, he proposed building a lobster cannery on Saint-Paul. The proposal was accepted—in part because the authorities considered it a matter of national interest to replace at least a fraction of the tons of canned lobster that France purchased from English factories with a domestic product. "Before long, Saint-Paul and Amsterdam will be colonized and will rise up like two cozy homes in the South Seas—a magnificent act of national expansion," claimed one French daily.

The first team of workers assembled a few precut wooden barracks with corrugated iron roofs on the northern shore of the crater inlet on Saint-Paul. The factory consisted of a main building with two annexes. The entire production process took place in these three buildings, up to and including the packing of the chunks of lobster in labeled cans. One year later, a second group arrived, with approximately one hundred colonists, including several children. The settlements reeked of garbage. Flayed penguin skins and lobster shells were everywhere, gnawed on by rats and surrounded by swarms of blue blowflies.

As had been arranged earlier, a ship came back just before the start of the southern summer to repatriate the workers. Seven volunteers were asked to stay behind to guard the installations: The lobster company would send another ship in three months to take supplies and deliver mail, and again three months after that to pick up the volunteers. One Malagasy and six Bretons offered to stay on: six men, three of whom were teenagers, and a pregnant woman, who refused to leave her husband.

The transport ship departed on the March 3, 1930. There appeared to be no shortage of provisions for the seven who would be staying behind. The storerooms were stocked with seventeen canisters of flour, countless cans of corned beef, six crates of canned sorrel and spinach, canned sardines, bouillon cubes, five bars of chocolate, a few packs of cookies, sugar, twenty-four pounds of coffee, and thirty cans of condensed milk. Some of the canned food turned out to have spoiled, and there was no cooking oil, but for that the island had its own sheep, goats, and ducks.

The married couple shared the little brick house next to the factory with Julien Le Huludut; the remaining four lived in a wooden barracks, fifty yards away. They slept next to one another on mattresses of cotton and seaweed. Three weeks after the ship left, the woman gave birth to a daughter: Paule. Five weeks later, the child's health began to fail, and at the end of May they had to bury her. One of the teenagers made the wooden cross.

The volunteers didn't plant any crops; they were fishermen and factory workers and knew nothing about agriculture. Even so, there was no danger of starving, as there was enough corned beef to last for months.

In the middle of May they began making daily visits to the island's highest point, where they would peer out over the sea. It wouldn't be much longer before the ship would arrive. But their isolation remained unbroken. The ship did not come in May, as had been agreed beforehand, or in June, or during the rest of the southern winter. The radio operator had left a short-wave radio in good condition, but it turned out that none of the islanders knew how to operate the machine. They were completely cut off from the outside world.

Emmanuel Pulloc'h came down with a fever. His gums became infected; his feet swelled up; he couldn't keep down any food; and on July 14 he became completely paralyzed. They put compresses on his head, but he died two weeks later, surrounded by his companions in misfortune. They buried him in a makeshift coffin. One of the Bretons recognized the symptoms. Looking in the medical handbook under "scurvy," he read: "Treatment consists primarily of eating fruit and fresh vegetables and drinking fresh squeezed orange and lemon juice."

Merciless winds came hurling off the high crater walls and sweeping across the tiny crater basin. By August, five months after the ship had left, all the forgotten inhabitants of Saint-Paul were weak and weary, and their legs were swollen. Refusing to touch the canned meat, they turned to fresh fish and penguin eggs, in the hope that their bodies would gradually recover from the lack of vitamins and the overdose of corned beef.

But the new diet didn't help. In late August the Malagasy died. One of the others wrote in his diary:

> A swelling so compressed his stomach that he practically suffocated. We kept watch by his bedside, picking him up and putting him on a chair so we could make his bed. Then when we turned around we saw he was no longer able to move. The only thing we could give him to drink was rainwater. We were there when it was over. He died in Le Huludut's arms.

At the beginning of the seventh month of their stay on Saint-Paul, the Brunous were unable to leave their bed. Louise recovered, but her husband was worn out. His legs swollen, he lay there for days, without moving or even speaking. He stared at the wall, his face completely blank. "He started to cry," Louis Herlédan wrote in his diary. "He was making a last effort to say something. We could read his lips: 'Not yet.'" The surviving inhabitants buried him across from the other graves, beside his daughter.

At the end of October, the eighteen-year-old Pierre Quillivic disappeared. On a day with a strong wind and high swells he had gone out in the motor boat, wearing his Breton clothes. He said he was going fishing despite the rough weather. At the two arms that mark the entrance to the caldera, his boat was swept out to the open sea. They never saw him again. Exactly what happened remained a mystery—perhaps he had engine trouble, but some thought that, in a fit of madness, Quillivic had sought to take refuge on Amsterdam, which they would have been able to see on clear days.

Finally, in early December, the boat arrived, six months late. The lobster company had suffered some financial setbacks, and in all that time no one had thought about the workers who had stayed behind on Saint-Paul.

They ship brought a new group of fishermen. Also on board was Louise Brunou's five-year-old daughter, who had been sent to her parents on Saint-Paul by unsuspecting relatives in Brittany. A photo has survived of the reunion: Mother and daughter are standing side-by-side behind the man-sized cross that marked the grave of their father and husband. Louise is wearing a tattered black coat. With folded hands she stares at the ground in grief. Her cheeks are hollow. The girl's round face peers inquisitively into the lens, while one arm dangles stiffly against her immaculate white skirt.

Thus at long last the three survivors were rescued, but incredibly Louise Brunou and Julien Le Huludut decided to sign a new contract and stay behind with the new arrivals. Apparently they just couldn't let go of Île Saint-Paul.

However, an outbreak of beriberi among the Malagasies on the island soon meant an enlargement of the cemetery by thirty graves—less than two months after the new fishermen had arrived—and the abandonment of the attempt to colonize Saint-Paul. Back in Brittany, Louise Brunou continued to yearn for Saint-Paul for the rest of her life; she longed to be able to stand at the graves of her husband and child. Perhaps she could no longer live without seclusion. In any case, she would never see the island again.

· · ·

When the *Marion Dufresne* had dropped anchor at Saint-Paul on its way to Amsterdam, I had searched for their graves. I found one moldering cross. The only other testaments to the past were the thousands of rusty tin lids that still littered the northern shore.

Amsterdam, by contrast, honored its dead. Their names lived on as craters or anchorages; at very least they were engraved on the monument near the overgrown gardens. The white cement sculpture consisted of a perpendicular wall, with a higher section jutting out from the center. The base of the monument was a favorite sleeping place for young seals. Most of the dead were buried in France. Carrying corpses aboard a ship is taboo for Malagasies, so the bodies were hidden in the container with the frozen aurochs meat without telling the crew.

It was a matter of record that Ribault and Antonelli had been killed in accidents, and that the Blue Monk and a former district chief had committed suicide. The meteorological technician Jacques Escarmant had died of a stroke, according to the Southern Lands newsletter, which "he had while sitting at his desk, after which he fell into a coma and slowly wasted away in the hospital." Robert Julo had drowned while out fishing, and adjunct chief meteorological technician Chedhomme had disappeared without a trace "while exploring the coast." A small hill with the grand name Chedhomme's Massif was the only reminder of him on the island.

Amsterdam and the other islands of the Southern Lands seemed to exert a magical attraction for people with suicidal tendencies. On the *Marion Dufresne* I had met a former district chief of the Crozet Islands, who had once been confronted with such a case. "It was a young guy who'd already spent one winter there," he said. "He'd signed a new contract to return to Crozet, but then he disappeared on his second day back. He left a suicide note. His body was never found." On another occasion, the same district chief of Crozet had been able to intervene. "The kid was at the end of his rope. In my opinion he was suicidal. He always wore a bright red jacket and sunglasses. I had him locked up and repatriated. You know, out here little problems can quickly get out of hand. Everything gets blown out of proportion because there's no corrective influence from the outside."

The islands were also a hotbed of rumors, at least one of which proved not entirely unfounded: the existence of a secret wine cellar on Amsterdam. Clammy, who had been on the island twenty-six years before, was the only one who knew where it was. As proof, he gave me a twenty-year-old bottle of wine that had been decanted into bottles on Amsterdam, a heavy Bordeaux with a strong, mossy bouquet, which I shared with the American and Kaplan.

Some of the men also spoke of secret ritual meetings between Bonbon and the American in the grassy interior of Dumas Crater. There were rumors that someone was stealing chocolate from the dining hall and that high-ranking officials of the Southern Lands were plotting to get rid of the current administrateur. Others were certain that, in order to cut costs, there were top-secret plans to evacuate the capital and abandon Amsterdam to the mercy of the elements. Or to turn it over to Australia, which was supposedly interested in taking over the weather station.

The most stubborn of these rumors was also the darkest—that one of the men who had died since the base was built had allegedly been murdered. The aerometric specialists passed on the story among themselves, as did the meteorologists and the biologists, always adding that it had never been proven, and that you should keep it to yourself.

But as much as the memory of the dead was kept alive, what truly dominated Amsterdam was the timelessness of the present. The west winds left few traces of the past. To the right of the monument to the dead were the foundations of the house of the reclusive Heurtin family. Old bottles had been found at various places around the island, and on the north shore lay the remains of a mast. In and around the capital the trappers and fishermen had carved their names in the rocks. A large part of the other inscriptions was in French, and dated from the years just after Heurtin had left the island. It seemed that the first inhabitant had wanted to hide the failure of his experiment from his countrymen by telling of the rich fishing grounds and fertile land. In the bushes along the boulevard Martin-de-Viviès, not far from the signpost, was the anchor of the *Vellore*, a three-master from Bordeaux that had been wrecked on the island. Clammy told me that you could still see the names of the survivors carved into a rock at Cape Recherche. So I decided to go there in the hope of finding those last signs of life.

. . .

It was actually against the rules to go to Cape Recherche on your
own, but the district chief let me go, provided I left as early as possible. A few days after my stint as a nurse, I left the capital at eight
o'clock in the morning via the western path, past the concrete circular heliport and the sign BIENVENUE À AMSTERDAM. At the cowline was a gate on which someone had painted the road sign for
"highway." The aerometric specialists used this path every day to
commute to work—one hour there, and one hour back. Even
though it was probably the busiest route on the island, it was also
the most problematic: From the cowline to the Virgin, the trail ran
straight through area inhabited by the reject fur seals. Every non-
breeding seal had marked off his territory with urine and other
filth, and the path was part of this hard-fought and painstakingly
partitioned ground. The biologists would sometimes crawl up to a
seal on their bellies; some of the animals would even let you pet
them. But this ritual could take as long as half an hour, and on a
path with dozens of seals, there was simply not enough time.

The seals have a distinct body language. The tensing of the chest
muscles and the retracting of the neck were the first signs of alert-
ness; this is to appear as massive as possible. Next, the animal might
next raise itself up, with its head in an almost vertical position, to
assert his dominance over the territory. But you weren't really in
trouble unless a male seal began to bark aggressively and dropped to
his belly, with its head pointed at you, the hostile, and its foreflippers
held as far back as possible, to keep them away from enemy teeth.

You could easily avoid an attacking seal by simply retreating,
but the problem was that this meant you would automatically step

into the territory of his neighbor. So it was possible that a passer-by might be hemmed in by various angry male seals, growling and baring their teeth.

I carefully passed the seals, stepping out of their way several times. Two radio towers were perched on the mountainside, over a primeval landscape with fragments of black lava that unfolded before me as far as the eye could see. A side path led to the north-ernmost point of the island, which everyone called the Virgin. The official name was Cape Goodenough, after the British naval cap-tain who had explored the northern coast 120 years earlier. This expedition had resulted in the first complete map of Amsterdam, which depicted the island as a rectangle with a regular, conical peak—a representation that bore no resemblance to reality.

No one on Amsterdam ever used the name Goodenough. This was not just because he was British; the main reason was that, at the end of the path, on the northernmost cliff on the island, there was a white statue of the Virgin Mary, with a weather-beaten clay tile where the only legible words were "thank," "cross," and "Jesus." The Virgin had become something of a site for pilgrims; the handy-men from Réunion in particular were in the habit of laying flowers there and praying for salvation. Farther on was a bay with a beach, littered with giant black boulders—wild, and virtually inaccessible. On top of the cliff with the statue was a rope you could use to lower yourself down, but I decided to return to the main path.

Fifteen minutes later I reached a small building with two aeromet-ric towers—one of two places on earth for measuring long-term pollution. Amsterdam was located within a zone of air masses that circled the Antarctic Region—ocean air virtually unimpeded by land and uninfluenced by people. The air on Amsterdam was some of the cleanest on earth. Kaplan and Pigpen recorded the carbon dioxide levels, in the lower atmosphere, the ozone levels, and, every twenty minutes, the radioactivity.

"No nuclear test in the southern hemisphere escapes our notice," said Kaplan.

"The whole island runs on the importance of our data," said Pigpen. "We can sell this information anywhere. Of course it's interesting to prove that a penguin can dive to depths of three hundred yards, but that doesn't really get you anything."

Their greatest threat was wind coming across the island, from the southeast, which was tainted by rotting animal carcasses and feces-ridden beaches. In their logbook they noted all events that could possibly influence the data. "9:30: tractor leaves boulevard for transmitting towers. 10:00: tractor returns." They also recorded the meteorologists' barbecues and passing ships. But all their detailed observations for an entire year easily fit inside a single notebook.

About half a mile past the aerometric towers, the path suddenly came to an end. I clambered over the slopes, which were covered with various low grasses, down to the sea. A whiff of fur seal life blew in my direction. I preferred the albatrosses: civilized, elegant, and calm. I reached the rocky shoreline, puzzled as to where Cape Recherche actually was. I soon found a tower of stacked rocks, but there was no trace of inscriptions from castaways. I walked on over the boulders. In the distance I spotted the hazy, massive contours of Mount Fernand. I stared at the lone, tormented rocks jutting out into the sea, two of which were big enough to have names: Durandal and the Loner. The surf pummeled away at them with great force, but time and again they emerged from the waves, apparently unscathed.

The sea was restless. I turned my gaze to the swiftly moving clouds and tried to recognize the birds flying overhead. Yellow-nosed albatrosses were black and white; Amsterdam albatrosses were larger and gray, and wandering albatrosses were white.

After fifteen minutes of searching I came across another pile of rocks marking the black slab of lava in which the inscriptions were carved. The *Vellore* had left Bordeaux on June 13, 1865, under the command of Captain Didier, bound for Batavia; on September 2 of that same year, the ship struck the rocks of Cape Recherche, with seventeen men on board. That was all that was known about the wreck of the three-master.

Just below the date of the accident, five men, including the captain, had inscribed their names. The sixth had only managed to carve an F. I ran my fingers over the rock. Did "F" die with the chisel in his hand? Was he washed to sea at that very moment? Had he and the other castaways run off cheering because a ship had appeared on the horizon? How many men had drowned, and did the survivors ever succeed in getting off the island? These were questions without answers.

I could plow my way through musty archives in port cities to see if I could find any leads. But what would be the point of trying to reconstruct all this? My folder labeled "Shipwrecks on Amsterdam" was already bursting with information.

In late January the weather on Amsterdam began to turn summery, with pleasantly warm patches suddenly popping up between the drizzles and the downpours. There were still a few streams and waterfalls, but in the coming weeks, evaporation would gain the upper hand, and almost all of these would dry up.

I went out with the Dreamer and Bonbon, who wanted to take advantage of the warm weather and go diving by the pier. The Dreamer didn't trust the seals, and wound up going back to the base to fetch a broomstick, which he used to gently disperse the creatures. A few sea elephants could be found on either side. These huge animals are the ugliest in the sea. The biggest males grow to twenty feet long and can weigh more than four tons. Their snorting nostrils are the size of Ping-Pong balls. A sheepdog could easily fit into their open mouths. Their little trunks could swell up, and their penises looked like vacuum cleaner hoses.

Their colonies were in the polar region. The ones who visited the jetty were mainly males who had come to Amsterdam to relax and recover from some brutal fight. Most of them had bite wounds or other disfigurements. Some were molting, with outer layers of skin hanging off them in tatters. They had nothing to fear here. Long ago, after the trappers nearly exterminated the fur seals, they switched to extracting sea elephant blubber by boiling the animals in grated cauldrons, but that was all ancient history.

I borrowed the Dreamer's wetsuit and snorkel while he and Bonbon kept chasing seals off the pier. Only one refused to budge; he was big and old, with half-closed eyes. With some difficulty I walked across the slippery rocks in my flippers. The swells were high. As soon as I could, I swam away from the beach to calmer waters. I was immediately surrounded by fur seals, who looked at me curiously and followed me around. In the water they were very social. They had no territory to defend there: The sea belonged to everyone.

Even some ways from the rocks, the waves were high. I felt myself getting seasick and soon headed back. I felt embarrassed in front of the Dreamer; I spent more time getting in and out of the wetsuit than swimming in the water.

After that I passed the whole afternoon hanging out in the shed where Bonbon, the Dreamer, and Longhaired Nico practiced new Lou Reed numbers every day. I had found my friends and my acquaintances on the island. I felt accepted and even surrounded with love, but I still often preferred to go off on my own.

Since my first visit, I had returned to the phylica forest countless times. I had my regular rock on a slope just past Dumas Crater, where I read and wrote. The place I was looking for had to meet a number of demands: The capital had to be invisible and inaudible, the view of the sea unobstructed, and there couldn't be any trace of humans.

It took me a month to discover the best spot for my reverie, just about five hundred yards from my room. To get there I went to the communal drying field, which served as the trailhead for my path. I climbed over the steel wire that had been strung up there a short time earlier to keep out Annabelle. The rocks beyond the laundry had the most inscriptions. I found the names of James Foster, John Rogers, and J. Bernardt, crew members of the American whaler *Tuscany*, which had been wrecked on Amsterdam. "TUSCANY OF SAG HARBOR LOST Here FEB 15 1855, IN MEMO-RIAM J & S."

The survivors of the disaster had managed to get off the island, I knew, because a newspaper on Mauritius had reported in April of that same year:

> *Shortly before the wreck of the Tuscany, while the crew was fish-ing, Captain White and his third officer had gone ashore, osten-sibly to get wood for a mast, but in reality to look for hidden treasure that was supposedly buried there. We have no evidence that their search was successful, but we have been informed that the third mate was in possession of a large quantity of half crowns following his time on Amsterdam.*

It was 76.8 degrees, one of the highest temperatures ever recorded on Amsterdam, according to the meteorologists, and this was in spite of the fact that they had been predicting a heavy rainstorm for four days. I'd decided to just put up with the sharp rocks and gravel; I slipped on my sandals, and headed off to my new spot. The path wound around the rocks and the occasional sleeping seal. The breeders and many of the females had left the island for a long stay in the sea, until their reproductive hormones started raging again and called them to the security of dry land. Only the frustrated males stayed behind, wounded or molting. There they lay for weeks, dejected, without eating or drinking.

I turned up my Walkman and glanced out at the sea. The path started out horizontal, and then, a bit farther down, made a sharp turn. Some hundred yards farther on, it merged with the main shoreline trail, which in turn ran about a third of a mile before dead-ending at the Ribault cabin.

I sat down on my regular "beach chair," which was partly formed of rushes that had molded to the shape of my back from the constant sitting. Since I'd started going there I had twice seen someone approaching in the distance. A strange sensation: Although I couldn't tell exactly who it was at that distance, I was sure it was a man, and what's more, someone I knew.

There was a gentle breeze. The sky was a hazy blue marked with a few vague, wafer-thin white streaks. The sea was calm; a few fleecy clouds hung low and motionless over the horizon. If I didn't know better, it could have been an island in the Mediterranean, but one that was untouched, safeguarded from tourists, including the most tenacious backpackers.

I put a Suzanne Vega tape in my Walkman and stared out at the sea. It was hot. I took off my clothes; the sun beat down on my body. I lay on my back in the rushes and closed my eyes.

Before me I saw the straight, endless country roads, which Eva and I had traversed every year with the sunroof open. Those were hot southern summers, and we listened to the tapes Eva had compiled with a mix of songs about trains, highways, or cities.

We swam in reservoirs, made love in stifling hotel rooms, and cherished the stickiness of our bodies. We wandered aimlessly through the wheat fields, and I had never been happier.

It had all just sort of happened, casually but irreversibly. We had gotten together to talk some more about our plan to set up a housing co-op. One summery day she sat on the couch in the living room of my humid basement apartment, wearing a white T-shirt. Eva was living with André, a war correspondent, every bit as dominant as she was. Their relationship was on the rocks. For months he had been following a guerrilla group in El Salvador; toward the end, Eva had only been getting short, impersonal letters and roll after roll of photographs showing corpses and hacked-off body parts. He was supposed to be coming back that week.

I'd known Eva for two years, but at that point I still didn't know

I loved her. We'd never so much as touched each other. On an impulse I asked her if she'd like to go to Normandy with me. She agreed without a moment's hesitation. Then we went to a café in the park and downed a bottle a wine.

We left the next morning. In France, we roamed across the rural byways, first following Eva's precise navigation with the map, and later according to my system—at every intersection take the most insignificant-looking turnoff and see where you end up.

We were in the middle of our first water-tower-counting contest when we were caught off-guard by the light fading away over the hills. In the dark I drove onto an unpaved path. I stopped and looked into the eyes of the woman who would be mine. We didn't let go of each other the whole night long.

The next morning we rolled down the steamed-up windows and found that we were parked next to a cemetery.

André came back; Eva left him immediately and hid out at a girl-friend's. The first night after she left, he started tossing all their furniture out of their third-story window, until the police intervened. Later that week he forced his way into Eva's friend's house after throwing a cobblestone through the windows. I was visiting Eva at the time, and André punched me out. When I got home I found some graffiti smeared across the front of my house, big letters in white paint: "And to think I loved you both so much—my God."

André's most subtle revenge consisted of the radio reports he filed as a war correspondent from the Bekaa Valley in Lebanon, where his means of transportation was a lazy, stubborn, and, above all, stupid donkey, paid for by his employers. He had to beat and kick the beast to get it moving. André had named the donkey Alfred.

. . .

The co-op was a reality. Eva and I had our own flats. She had short hair that she dyed blond; she didn't shave her armpits.

We dreamt about someday moving to a village in the south, to a house with a panoramic view of parched hills, where bougainvillea grew and the nights were damp. We felt we were soul mates.

Eva began wearing short skirts; she made a career for herself as a photographer and an expert on incest. She taught me how to notice things. We took the trips we had always dreamed of taking; together we picked out "designer" doorknobs. The co-op grew, one by one the others started pairing off, and in time the first children were born.

Eva was the first to bring the subject up, but I said I still wasn't ready. But that didn't keep us from talking about names for several nights. We agreed on a boy's name right away. I had no brothers, no uncles, no cousins. My family tree had been uprooted: I was the last branch. My great-grandfather was named Jacob, my grand-father Samuel, my father Jacob, and my name was Alfred Samuel. If Eva and I had a son, his name would be Jacob Elias: Jacob after his grandfather, and Elias after the gravedigger "from the Toll Bridge on the Amstel," who was the first member of the family to reach the outskirts of the city.

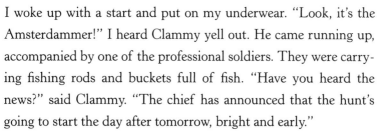

I woke up with a start and put on my underwear. "Look, it's the Amsterdammer!" I heard Clammy yell out. He came running up, accompanied by one of the professional soldiers. They were carrying fishing rods and buckets full of fish. "Have you heard the news?" said Clammy. "The chief has announced that the hunt's going to start the day after tomorrow, bright and early."

I froze. The district chief had already asked me several times to come along: "That's part of life on Amsterdam; you can't say no. But you won't have to carry a rifle if you'd rather not, or bone the meat." I had promised to go, and now there was no getting out of it.

I waited for the sun to go down. The sky turned a purplish red. I put on my clothes and went back to my room at the Tern. The cook rang the dinner bell.

Early the next afternoon the Chimney, the Slaughterer, the American, Bonbon, and Jeff assembled at the residence. Jeff, a professional soldier, had gotten decked out in military garb for the occasion: camouflage outfit, military beret, Sam Browne belt, boots, and dark sunglasses.

212 ALFRED VAN CLEEF

I was not the only one on the island who didn't have to shoot. Like the other "vacationers," I was exempt; everyone who was staying the winter was required to participate in the hunt at least once. As head game warden and biologist, the district chief was the leader of the expedition. He had been there ten years earlier when the part of the herd that lived south of the fence had been exterminated. The man had shot nine hundred cows in six weeks.

We climbed into two fifty-year-old jeeps; apart from the similarly ancient Caterpillar used by the volunteer fire department, these were the only automobiles on the island. One of the ATVs was painted with wild black and white stripes; APOCALYPSE COW was written in big letters on the back. The vehicle had been converted into a mobile fighting unit. The open bed had a pulley-driven hoist for lifting the carcasses on board; two plastic chairs were fastened to the roof. The American and Jeff were sitting in them, their rifles at the ready. The hard part of the hunt was hauling away the dead cows. Sometime in the past, reservoirs had been dug out alongside the two main paths, to lure thirsty cows close to the edge of the road, where they could be killed. But the project had ended in failure: The cows had avoided the reservoirs, as if they saw through the hunters' plans.

We drove to the Antonelli cabin, where we would be spending the night. We stayed on the unpaved path for as long as possible; after that, the ATVs crawled over the steep, rocky slopes toward the edge of the crater. When we reached the cabin, the Slaughterer roasted some fish on the grill. After dinner the district chief and the Chimney got into an argument about how to deal with the shortage of chocolate spread.

"We need stricter rules," said the Chimney. "We have to impose a maximum quantity per day, per person, and be strict about checking to make sure no one takes any more."

These were the words of a soldier. The chief disagreed with him completely: "Everyone should be able to eat whatever he likes for breakfast. And if we run out of chocolate spread someday, that's too bad. But at least you'll get a decent amount for several weeks instead of having too little every day."

I passionately supported the chief, even though I was the only one on the island who preferred cheese on his bread to chocolate.

We went to bed early. At four o'clock in the morning the district chief gave the starting signal. He and the American first looked for cows on the slopes to the right of us, but they didn't find any. After that they headed to the other side. Suddenly they saw two bulls, an old one and a young one. The American and the chief crept up on them; I had to stay at a distance. Sometimes the hunters would shoot close to the settlement. In view of the risk this entailed, the chief had imposed a general curfew for the capital.

The chief was the first to shoot; the young bull fell down dead. The American wounded the other bull. It thrashed around desperately three or four times, until the chief put him out of his misery.

The potbellied Slaughterer came running up with his set of knives; the Chimney was already next to the dead bulls. The Slaughterer removed the old bull's testicles. "So they don't get in the way." He cut open the belly, stuck his hand inside, and cut out the fourth stomach: "This is for the birds and blowflies."

The bulls were hoisted by the head onto Apocalypse Cow and driven to the open-air abattoir located on the south side of the capital, next to the chicken run. The carcasses hung there on meat hooks. Kaplan and two other aerometrics specialists cut the meat into pieces with razor-sharp knives and a circular saw. The blood gushed over them, staining their white jackets. The skins and tails lay on the ground, the two heads next to the path. In the streets of the capital the sweet smell of the male seals mingled with the odor of fresh meat. The meat supplies were back up to their usual level, although that proved little help to Annabelle. Her presence on the base had once again become untenable. Two new attempts to resettle the calf across the cowline failed, because she kept jumping the barbed wire and running back to the boulevard. The chief decided to take firm action. He recruited the Chimney, the Slaughterer, and a few professional soldiers. Under escort, Annabelle was led off to the abattoir. The Dreamer walked away in anger.

The Slaughterer killed the animal at once and then boned it. The meat was stored in the refrigerators. The chief assured us that no one on Amsterdam would be getting pieces of Annabelle on his dinner plate; he would personally see to it that the meat was exported to the other southern districts.

For weeks the chief had been charting the *Marion Dufresne's* progress on the blackboard in the dining hall. Up to Crozet, everything had gone according to schedule, but at Kerguelen harbor the ship had lost some of its freight during a storm and had been delayed for three days. According to the latest calculations it would be another two weeks before the *Marion* reached Amsterdam.

We were given the choice between an apple and a semisoft kiwi; after that there would be no more fruit. Once again accusations flew about theft and excessive consumption of chocolate spread. The latter, which most of the men considered an indispensable part of breakfast, had become so scarce that the cook had secreted the remaining two half-full jars somewhere in the kitchen, and only brought them out on special occasions.

I was finally going to take the trek of treks; it was my last chance. The American had just returned from d'Entrecasteaux; I asked him, the experienced mountain climber, how it had been: "Hell. The wind up there's horrendous, and there are pools of mud several yards deep. Still, it's more than worth the effort. But you'll have to keep plugging away at a pretty good pace if you don't want to run into trouble."

I'd already put off the chance once before to take the same hike. It was a grueling daylong march across dangerous terrain—followed by a long rappel down with ropes and pitons. The fact that even the American, with his well-trained body, thought it was hard did not bode well for me.

Sensing my hesitation, he offered to accompany me and David, who had also signed up, as far as the cabin. After that he'd head back to the capital with one of the aerometric specialists and the cook, who would be just finishing their stay at d'Entrecasteaux. The plan was pretty daring; as far as anyone knew, he'd be the first person to go to the secluded bay and back in one day. But the district chief consented.

David and I would spend four days in the cabin with Louis and the Ascetic, who had already been there for some time. Because Louis's birthday happened to fall during that period, we took two bottles of wine from the kitchen. I had a heavy load to carry: extra clothing, mountain climbing helmet, sleeping bag, and provisions, along with some fresh supplies that had been ordered by the biologists.

We left very early the next day. It was dry and partly cloudy. There was a stiff southwesterly wind, which made it feel colder than the 53 degrees indicated by the thermometer.

We climbed toward the cowline. David and I were struggling. The American kept disappearing from sight, but would always wait patiently for us to catch up. The lowland slopes were covered with thistles; other plants had less chance of surviving the grazing cattle. The ground was loose; we were careful where we placed our feet. I tried to maintain a steady pace and not look up to see how far it was. Near the Cyclops I found my cadence; I felt free.

I passed a cow carcass: the stench was powerful, but didn't carry far. Similar emaciated carcasses could be found all across the island, covered with blowflies. This was particularly true in the summertime, when the lowlands dried out and the half-starved cows were too weak to look for food. After a few months nothing was left but bones and a tanned hide. Eventually only the bones remained, and they could be found in the farthest corners of the island, white and odorless.

When we reached the cowline, we found the American waiting for us on a boulder. There was a wooden step to help you over the barbed wire, but all the strength seemed to have drained from my muscles, so I couldn't lift my leg. It wasn't until the American took my rucksack that I managed to make it over.

We followed the trail up, first through the toadrush and other marsh plants that covered the lower hills, and after that over the springy mosses of the highland, which was covered with exotic ferns. After climbing seven hundred yards, we reached the virgin ground of the Moorland Plateau: forever in the clouds, damp, vulnerable. We walked around the edge of the caldera and stopped at the foot of Mount Dives. We had a little bit to eat and drink, then donned our waders and waterproof jackets, sealing off the openings with duct tape.

The path ran into a deep gully that led to a gurgling, sucking marsh. The American just scrambled across on his hands and knees, but David and I could hardly make any progress at all. If you didn't pull out your leg after each step, you sank to your thighbones in the mire. On two occasions, both my arms and legs got stuck, and I fell face-first into the mud. David and I decided to cut across the rare, endemic mosses: The American didn't seem the least bit bothered by this forbidden assault on the ecosystem.

The marsh stopped at the Rabbit Pool. Over the summit of the Gable, the clouds were scattering at great speed. Within thirty seconds everything was clear, and the light was sharp and unfiltered. The view of the ocean was exceptionally clear. A brown prominence pierced the clouds on the horizon, with a slanted white plume: Saint-Paul. It was a magical moment. Although the island was fifty miles away and unreachable, I couldn't take my eyes off it. For the first time since my arrival on Amsterdam there was visible evidence of a world outside.

We made for the Gable, which, along with Mount Fernand and the Railing, formed the last remaining rims of the original volcano, the rest of it having fallen into the sea thousands of years ago. I had a view of the impressively steep, black-green slopes of Cape d'Entrecasteaux. Below, in the depths, a wide strip of sea foam marked the winding coastline, which stretched as far as the Cathedral. And straight ahead of the enormous rock was the bay where we would be spending the night: hazy, virginal, like a secret cove, which only a select few were permitted to look upon.

At the Dining Hall, a sharp pinnacle at the top of the descent, we met the cook and the aerometric expert. Their faces were covered in sweat; they were recuperating from having just climbed up the cliff, together with Louis. We ate our sandwiches.

The bay had always been a paradise that was virtually inaccessible by land and probably from the sea as well. The one exception was Wolf Fish Inlet, a small, concealed beach east of the Cathedral. It did not seem impossible that Willem de Vlamingh had come ashore there. I had a photograph of d'Entrecasteaux Bay that had been taken from the sea, just offshore from the Cathedral: a dizzying vertical slope that seems to crash into the ocean but then suddenly sprouts another outcropping, a replica of itself in miniature.

It was not until the early 1970s that the first scientists dared to venture into the ravine. So the El Dorado of Amsterdam had actually never been visited by the man for whom it was named: Admiral Antoine de Brunei, Chevalier d'Entrecasteaux. He had been sent out with two flute-ships to look for the Count de La Pérouse and his squadron, who had been missing for three years.

On March 28, 1792, d'Entrecasteaux explored the southwestern coast of Amsterdam, under a gray sky. The island was covered with thick clouds, with the mountaintops barely peeking through. "After four hours we were close enough to determine that it was smoke," wrote d'Entrecasteaux in his log. The forest was on fire, and it was easy to follow the course of the blaze.

Some of the crew members wondered if the fire had "originated in the bowels of the earth," or whether it might be the result of a rescue signal started by stranded sailors that had gotten out of hand, but d'Entrecasteaux didn't believe either explanation. Even assuming that the hypothetical castaways had spotted the two flutes the moment they appeared on the horizon, there was no way they could have set off a fire of that magnitude. The admiral also doubted that a permanent fire would be raging on an island that no one ever visited.

The fire appeared to have done most damage to the north coast.

The thick smoke had caused cumulus clouds to form, in shades of gray ranging from off-white to almost black, depending on which part of the fire they came from. After sunset, the island was illuminated by a ghostly light, and the skies had a coppery glow, as just before the outbreak of a violent storm. Not far from the conflagration, d'Entrecasteaux gave the order to raise the sails. "We were soon surrounded by clouds so thick they almost completely obscured the flames. We didn't extricate ourselves from the fog until we had sailed out to five fathoms. It smelled of forests and scorched earth," he later wrote.

D'Entrecasteaux's motto was "Nothing but sea and a bit of glory"—but in the end, his voyage failed to bring him much of the latter. He found no trace of the lost expedition. After the French admiral left Amsterdam, he sailed past the Santa Cruz Islands in the South Pacific. Later reports by other travelers would place his ship just a few miles from the site of the shipwreck. And to add insult to injury: The wreckage had been found by an English captain.

The American had initially planned to fly to d'Entrecasteaux in his hang glider, but the district chief had forbidden it. Although he didn't need to climb down with us, there was nothing he would rather do. He asked the aerometric expert and the cook to wait for him at the Dining Hall.

We put on our helmets. Mine wobbled a bit, but if I tightened the clasp, it was too tight. The first section of the long descent (over two thousand feet) consisted of a steep, gravely path. Some sharp rocks gave me my first few scratches. After that I began rappelling, secured by climbing ropes and carabiners. The depths below were terrifying, and I tried to keep my eyes focused straight ahead. For the next part of the climb my only security was the climbing rope I held on to as I pushed off from the rocks. Dangling in the air, I felt my way down the face with my feet, in search of points of support.

I was relieved when I reached a narrow, grottolike cove. I hugged the rockface and carefully edged toward the precipice. In the winter a waterfall plunged past the same rocks, making a permanent climbing rope an impossibility. Instead, there was a rope ladder that wound its way around the rocks as far as the eye could see; the American claimed it had never been replaced. The danger was in the safety system. You had to unhook your carabiner while standing on one rung, and reattach it a few rungs down—which meant that you were constantly left hanging there, unsecured, with only one hand on the ladder.

"Unnecessary and unreliable," was the American's verdict, but his face was beaming. Here he was again, testing his own limits. I felt no fear; my only goal was to reach d'Entrecasteaux.

At the bottom of the rope ladder was a long, steep descent full of loose rocks, with a climbing rope as my only aid. I didn't know what to do with my feet. Then, a mud trail led us down to the very bottom. It smelled of salt and dead animals. The dominant sound was the roar of the breakers, on occasion drowned out by the hoarse barking of fur seals. We passed a few albatross nests, and after that the penguin beach. The narrow strip of coastline was littered with rubble and large boulders, and crisscrossed with deep crevices and mountain streams. I thought I had completed the ultimate journey, but I still had an arduous struggle through the brakes ahead, through rushes as tall as I was. It was perhaps another few hundred yards to the cabin, but on my last reserves of energy it took me half an hour to get there.

The cabin was called Among the Yellow-Noses. It was filthy: There were dead flies everywhere: on the counter, on the floor, in the makeshift washbasin. Thousands of them forced their way in through the screens all at once, only to drop to the ground almost immediately afterward and die a lingering death.

The cabin had a faucet that was connected to a barrel of water by a small hose. The source was only a half hour's walk away, but considering the effort required to drag a barrel of water over the rocks and through the brakes, the barrel was generally empty. Both Louis and the Ascetic reeked; they had been among the albatrosses and the penguins for two solid weeks and had seldom washed.

The Ascetic had been coming to d'Entrecasteaux for a year and a half, always with two or three others, on account of the safety regulations. It was clear that the cabin really belonged to him, though he assured us that the pinups on the wall had been put up by the previous resident. Still, he didn't seem to be the least bit bothered by the invasion of rucksacks and sleeping bags.

Louis and the Ascetic grabbed four randomly chosen ready-made dinners from the blue plastic barrels with screw-top lids that stood next to the cabin. The provisions were flown in once a year by helicopter; they were months and sometimes years past their use-by date. The Ascetic shook the dead blowflies out of the pan and dumped in the canned food. At the table the biologists talked about rat routes and albatross vomit. Some of their pastimes seemed a little strange, such as collecting penguin droppings and bird fleas.

For years the district chief had doubled as an exterminator.

After the aurochs had been decimated, he became obsessed with the rats. On Saint-Paul, with the help of a dog, he had managed to exterminate every last one of them. On Amsterdam that seemed to be impossible; the island was much too large, with too many inaccessible reaches. To deal with them effectively he had given the Ascetic the task of recording their habits as accurately as possible.

Next to the door were vile concoctions of moldy bread and rancid margarine, which the Ascetic used to lure rats for his research. He caught the animals in traps and tied a transmitter to them. With the help of a receiver he would wander the hillsides and comb the beaches every day from twelve to four in the afternoon and from midnight to four in the morning, in the hope that the receiver he lugged around with him would detect the presence of a rat.

They were in fact common gray rats, far removed from the sewers of their ancestors. Unable to compete with the rapacious great skuas and petrels, they had adapted and become vegetarians.

I awoke the next day with aching muscles. I went out to pee. The cries of the albatrosses rebounded off the Cathedral. The slopes of the Great Balcony were shrouded in fog; steep and intimidating.

After breakfast I sat for hours on a flat stone not far from the cabin. The sea, always the sea. I listened to the boulders as they rolled across the beach. The surf roared against the Cathedral, the bay's unapproachable sentry, the peak of which was toothed like a crown. Louis had shown me how you could discern figures in the rock, if you looked hard: two bearded savages and Charles de Gaulle.

Behind the penguin colony was a cliff still bearing the traces of last year's hurricane. The Ascetic had been there when waves of thirty or even fifty feet had ravaged d'Entrecasteaux Bay. Here and there you could still see the wreckage, but most of it had been permanently claimed by the sea; the shore looked as if it had been gnawed on by a giant excavator.

It was Louis's birthday. In the evening David and I took the wine out of our rucksacks; Louis conjured up a bottle of champagne and served duck pâté on antediluvian slices of toast. The Ascetic read a book while Louis, David, and I talked about life in the capital. "I'm happy every time I come here," said Louis. He felt that the atmosphere on the base was like being on board a submarine: "Suffocating."

At midnight, armed with a receiver and a miner's lamp, the Ascetic set out in the pouring rain in search of rats.

The next afternoon I went with Louis to the yellow-nosed albatross colony. We first walked to the edge of the Great Balcony, straight through the rushes. The slope before us was vertiginous, and was only manageable because the ground was covered with tall, marramlike grass, which you could use to pull yourself up.

Ninety percent of all yellow-nosed albatrosses in the world came from Amsterdam; they nested within a few yards of the same spot every year. Three of the eight colonies at Cape d'Entrecasteaux had been studied for twenty-five years. At a height of 650 feet we passed dozens of empty nests. Colony one had been the site of a disaster. "They left the whole thing behind, the unhatched eggs and the young," said Louis. "The chicks died of hunger. Massive desertions like that happen from time to time. No one knows why."

In the middle of the second colony we kept quiet. Together we weighed the young, which you could grab by the neck and place in a little basket. They were six weeks old on average, and wrapped in white down. Now and then an adult would land at one of the nests. They came flying in at a great speed and left skid marks on the ground, like birds in a cartoon. Sometimes they would spit up a pound of fish and shellfish into the beak of a chick. Two albatrosses were performing a courtship ritual, dancing around each other with clattering beaks and open wings.

The albatrosses glided through the air without moving their wings, except for when they took off. "Look, a sooty albatross couple flying in synch," Louis said as we sat down and looked out over the tranquil bay. "Those are practice flights. The males and the females have to be completely attuned to each other if they're going to form a couple. That's why their engagement takes so long. They do everything together, from incubating the egg to raising the chicks. They take turns feeding the young. Sometimes they cover more than five hundred hundred miles in a single day. They devote all their energy to reproduction, and they stay true to each other forever."

Louis had a joint with him, which we shared. For a moment I thought about telling him what was on my mind, but I said nothing and stared at the bay.

Eva and I hadn't wanted to get married, even if we had had children. We believed in our individual freedom—or at least that's what we told each other. We had separate bank accounts, our own dishes, our own lives. Ideally we only shared those experiences that were important to us as a couple: treks through deserts and forests of palm trees, a journalistic trip to some tropical slum, long walks through the fields.

But everything changed after that night in a Channel Island hotel room adorned with posters of Prince Charles and Lady Di. We almost came simultaneously, but I pulled out at the last minute because we weren't using a condom. Eva pushed me away with tears in her eyes. From that moment on we were united in our desire for children.

After a year we started getting impatient. We thought it was because Eva only had one fallopian tube. We went to a "woman-friendly" gynecologist. They would have to examine Eva's fallopian tube and test my sperm as well: "That's the standard procedure here."

. . .

"The test came out favorably," said the gynecologist. There was nothing wrong with Eva's fallopian tube; she should be able to conceive. We discussed Eva's results for a quarter of an hour.

"Yes, well, and then we have one more set of test results. The sperm . . ."

We stopped talking; Eva held my hand.

"Plainly put, there wasn't any," said the gynecologist. "Zero percent. We didn't find a single sperm cell."

Back in the car, we cried. We drove to the sea. We walked along the beach arm in arm, the wind in our faces. We didn't even have to say it. This was our battle, and we would fight it together.

Eva shared her sadness with her girlfriends. I started putting together a voluminous file, filled with scholarly articles, newspaper clippings, and reports of conversations I had had with various doctors. I remained optimistic about new medical techniques, and if that didn't work, I managed to resign myself to a life without progeny.

Eva's desire for children was as strong as ever. She couldn't feel complete as a woman unless she gave birth. The quest began to dominate her life. I realized that my position was fundamentally different: I had no choice but to accept that this was how I was. Eva still had a choice.

We rejected the idea of taking sperm from friends: They would end up getting involved with the child. In the end we decided to try our luck with artificial insemination using semen from an anonymous donor. I gently asked whether they might be able to find someone who also had family that had been in the train cars and—"We make our selections solely on the basis of appearance," said the woman at the sperm bank. "We choose the donor who looks the most like you."

She came back to that later. "I'm really not supposed to do this, but I wanted to do you a favor. I found someone with the background you desired, at least one quarter, anyway. And he's musical. I can't tell you any more than that."

We accepted the donor. I imagined a medical student with dirty blond hair—a violinist, perhaps—jerking off in one of the bare little rooms in the fertility laboratory to earn a little extra on the side. I knew those rooms well: the hospital beds, the fluorescent lights, the rolling nightstands with the well-thumbed porno magazines.

Every morning at six thirty Eva had to take her temperature; she was fanatical and never skipped a day. If she was fertile, we went to the woman-friendly gynecologist, who injected the semen with a straw. Sometimes we had to come back three or even five times a month.

With most women the procedure succeeded after a few cycles, but Eva simply didn't get pregnant. Not after four months, not after half a year. And not even when the musical donor dropped out and was replaced by another one, who, we were told, was not "exactly like" the first one.

We graduated from the private practice of the woman-friendly gynecologist to the hospital. The worst were the Saturdays, when we had to report to the department of obstetrics. We had to sit there in a room full of couples with prying eyes, all of whom had one thing in common: It wasn't working, and it was the man's fault. We often had to wait a long time for the gynecologist: Emergency deliveries took priority, we were told—we could certainly understand that.

When Eva still wasn't pregnant after a year and a half, we had to give up the fight. We felt ourselves growing further apart; it was as if the foundation had been knocked out of our relationship.

Eventually Eva moved out of my life. When I left she was living not far from me, with her new partner. Now and then I saw her on the street with her two daughters. They look like her.

The sun sank, setting the Cathedral on fire. "I haven't been twenty-two for more than a day, but I feel that I could die right here," said Louis. "A little bit higher up, there at the peak of the Railing. The rocks would take me."

By my last day at d'Entrecasteaux, I was completely filthy: We were out of water. I headed off to Wolf Fish Inlet. This was my last chance. If Willem de Vlamingh had come ashore somewhere other than the lava tongue near the capital, it could only have been at the small cove east of the Cathedral: On that side of the cliff, the surf wasn't as rough, and it was the only cove with an accessible beach.

I followed a worn little path toward my favorite flat stone, and found myself in the middle of the rockhopper colony. These were small penguins with two bright yellow plumes; they look like tropical hippies.

The colony was a whole village, complete with squares, streets and alleys, gossipy neighbors, and a network of roads separating inbound and outbound traffic. Some penguins sat high up on the slopes, as far as the Railing; every day they waddled down six hundred yards and then another six hundred yards back up. Rockhoppers are the only singing penguins; their cries are subdivided into numerical sequences like bar codes, which allows them to communicate their position, sex, and individual identity.

Does the information that is instinctively passed on from penguin to penguin have to do with the times when the old colonies by
the capital were destroyed by men in fur jackets? Does it recall the
souls of their ancestors, who were first beheaded with a scythe and
then crushed into liquid fuel in the "penguin press," a demonic
apparatus the invaders had brought with them in their ships? For
whatever atavistic reason they might have, the rockhoppers can fly
into a total panic at the slightest provocation, which often causes
the entire colony to flee.

I carefully made my way up along the tortuous penguin paths.
The bay was on the other side of the narrows connecting the
Cathedral to the foothills of the Railing and the Great Balcony.
Right by the peak was a strong wind, which carried the sickly odor
fur seals right toward me.

I crept to the edge and looked down. Wolf Fish Inlet was less
than a hundred yards long, and entirely surrounded by a wall over
two thousand feet high, leaning inward, with bands of black lava
running through it like highways observed from the air, complete
with on-ramps and overpasses.

Louis had told me it was possible to descend to the narrow
beach. "I've done it. You mainly hang from your hands. It's pretty
exciting." The climbing rope was attached to the outermost point
of the cliff. I glanced down. In the best-case scenario it would be a
week before a helicopter could pick me up. After that it would be
another week before I got to a real hospital. I stayed where I was
and took out my camera.

It might be possible to climb up at the corner by the Cathedral,
but given the difficulty, it was unlikely that De Vlamingh had
stopped here, at an unapproachable bay closed off from the rest of

the island. The beach appeared to be dotted with little black rocks, but when I took a good look, I saw that they were moving: seal pups. Wolf Fish Inlet was a nursery.

That night it stormed. You could hear the wind coming from far off: quiet at first, then gradually growing in intensity into a violent gale that tugged at the plastic barrels and the cabin. Creaking noises. "It'll be an athletic hike back tomorrow," said the Ascetic.

When I made it back to the capital I saw that a list of cabin assignments for the return trip had been posted near the foosball table in the Great Skua, alongside a list of passengers who would be spending the night on Amsterdam.

Of those who would be leaving the island, only David was enthusiastic: He was looking forward to seeing his pregnant girlfriend. The others kept to themselves, conscious of the impending collapse of their community and the abrupt disturbance of their self-imposed isolation; perhaps they also feared the renewed confrontation with cars, phones, and noise.

Days before the *Marion Dufresne* was due to arrive, there was a menacing, nervous atmosphere in the capital. Those scheduled for departure began packing their belongings into crates; those who were staying wrote letters to their loved ones: After seven weeks the post office was officially open again.

The question was: Did the *Marion* have mail on board? In the past there had been problems when the ship left Durban for the Southern Lands. Letters for the residents of Amsterdam were sent from Paris, with the address "Amsterdam, via *Marion Dufresne,*

Durban." The South African post offices had immediately forwarded the mail, and three days later the letters arrived in Amsterdam, Holland—at which point they were sent back to Paris.

The scientists counted, measured, and weighed everything they
had on hand; they drew up lists and filled in forms. They classified
whatever flotsam and jetsam had washed ashore as well as the various species of alga. They stored bird fleas and penguin droppings
in plastic bags. In their laboratory, the aerometrics experts packed
up the test tubes filled with rainwater for shipment to Paris.

At the invitation of the district chief, I wrote an entry in the
Golden Book: It was a lyrical description of the island and its
inhabitants. The three previous texts had all been written by the
administrateur who had so long opposed me.

The district chief might have been the harbormaster on an
island without a harbor, but that didn't stop him from discharging
his duty as thoroughly as possible. He had the strips of grass along
the boulevard mown, and ordered all litter to be picked up, all
streets to be swept, and the rooms made ready for the guests from
the *Marion Dufresne*. He personally painted all the lampposts
orange. "That brightens things up a bit."

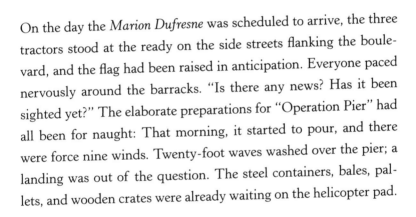

On the day the *Marion Dufresne* was scheduled to arrive, the three tractors stood at the ready on the side streets flanking the boulevard, and the flag had been raised in anticipation. Everyone paced nervously around the barracks. "Is there any news? Has it been sighted yet?" The elaborate preparations for "Operation Pier" had all been for naught: That morning, it started to pour, and there were force nine winds. Twenty-foot waves washed over the pier; a landing was out of the question. The steel containers, bales, pallets, and wooden crates were already waiting on the helicopter pad.

When the ship's horn finally sounded, the district chief returned the greeting by switching on the island's siren. After that we all started walking in the direction of the overgrown gardens, with the chief and the Chimney at the head of the group. We saw the ship appear; it dropped anchor at Ribault.

When the helicopter landed, we simultaneously turned our backs to the sea and closed our eyes to keep out the flying straw. I saw my first women in seven weeks, one of whom was a biologist I had met on the voyage out. It turned out that she had been buried

under falling rocks in a landslide on Crozet. Her arm was in a cast
and she had a neck brace; she was on her way to a hospital on the
mainland.

I escaped the invasion in the capital and followed the path to the
Ribault cabin. For the last time I sat down at my regular spot; I
didn't care about getting soaked. I stared at the gray sea and cried.

Toward evening the weather cleared, but by the time I got up
the next morning it had again started to rain. In our sou'westers we
walked to the helicopter. I hugged Bonbon and the other meteorologists, the handymen and Louis, and climbed in. From the sky I
had one final glimpse of the Great Skua, the residence, the Malagasy Gardens, and the seals, who, frightened by the noise, slid off
the lava spit into the sea.

I stood on the afterdeck, away from the others. Albatrosses and
petrels followed the boat. The higher slopes were veiled by clouds;
only a narrow strip of land was visible. The colors were the first
thing to disappear. For a second I caught sight of two waterfalls
and the silhouette of Dumas Crater. Then the island vanished into
the mists, and there was nothing more to see.

Bibliography

Sources used for the description of Willem de Vlamingh's voyage to Amsterdam, 1696:

Robert, Willem C. H. *The explorations, 1696–1697, of Australia by Willem de Vlamingh.* Amsterdam: Philo Press, 1972.

Schilder, G. G., and De Linschoten-vereeniging. *De ontdekkingsreis van Willem Hesselsz. de Vlamingh in de jaren 1696–1697.* The Hague: Martinus Nijhoff, 1976.

The citations are taken from the following ships' logs, which were printed in the aforementioned scholarly works:

Hardenbergh, Gerrardt. *Journael gehouden nopende de siecken en patieenten voorgekomen op de reyse van Texel tot aen de Caep de Gode Hoop onder handen van mey Gerrardt Hardenbergh, oppermeester op' t schip de Geelvinck, gecomandeert door commandeur Willem de Vlamingh ten dienst der genereaele geoctrojeerde Oostindische Compagnie ter kaemer Amsterdam.* 1696.

Torst, Mandrop. *Journaal wegens een voyagie gedaan op order der Hollandsche Oost-Indische Maatschappy in de Jaaren 1696 en 1697 door de hoekerscheepje de Nyptangh, het schip de Geelvink, en het galjoot de Wezel, na het onbekende Zuidland, En wyders na Batavia, Amsterdam.* 1701.

Vlamingh, Willem de. *Anno 1696. Gedachtenisse der voornemelykste bevindingen int vergat de Geelvink door mij Willem de Vlamingh, gedestineert*

naer *Zuijtlant en vooreerst de eijlanden Tristant de Conha, St.Pouwel en Amsterdam aen te doen, God verleent ons geluck en behoude rijs.* Copy of the journal kept by Commander Willem de Vlamingh on the *Geelvinck* from August 17, 1696, to March 20, 1679.
The quote by Nicolaas Witsen, mayor of Amsterdam, is taken from Nicolaas Witsen, "Uittreksel uit een brief van burgemeester Nicolaas Witsen aan dr Martin Lister, Amsterdam, 3 oktober 1698," in: *Philosophical Transaction: giving some account of the present undertakings, studies and labours of the ingenious, in many considerable parts of the world. Vol XX for the year 1698.* London: printed for S. Smith . . . MDCXCIX; reprinted in G.G. Schilder and De Linschotenvereeniging. *De ontdekkingsreis van Willem Hesselsz. de Vlamingh in de jaren 1696–1697* (see above).

The watercolors of Amsterdam Island by Victor Victorsz. are the property of the Prince Hendrik Maritime Museum, Rotterdam, where they are held in repository.

Additional Literature

Alderley, Lord Stanley of. *The first Voyage round the world, by Magellan, translated from the accounts of Pigafetta and other writers by-.* London: Hakluyt Society, 1874.
Allègre, Jean-Luc. *Terres australes et antarctiques françaises.* Saint-Paul and Réunion: Editions Jean-Luc Allègre, September 1997.
Arnaud, Patrick M., and Jean Beurois. *Les armateurs du rêve. Les concessions Bossière et les sociétés françaises d'exploitation des îles australes de l'océan Indien (1893–1939).* Marseille: Mme F. Jambois, 1996.
Aubert, Michel. "L'établissement de la Nouvelle-Amsterdam." *Revue TAAF,* no. 6 (1958).
Aubert de la Rüe, E. "Les années tragiques de l'île Saint-Paul (1928–1931) et quelques aperçus historiques de la pêche autour de l'île." *Revue TAAF,* nos. 55–56 (ca. 1971).
Ben, Dominique. *Lettre AMAPOF,* 29 (January 1991).
Bénard, Robert, ed. *Mémoires du capitaine Péron sur ses voyages aux côtes d'Afrique, en Arabie, à l'Ile d'Amsterdam, aux îles d'Anjonau et de Mayotte, aux côtes nord-ouest de l'Amérique, aux îles Sandwich, à la Chine.* Facsimile edition. Bibliotheca Australiana nos. 69 en 70. Israel/Da Capo: Amsterdam, 1971.

Berteaux, D. "Female-biased mortality in a sexually dimorphic ungulate: feral cattle of Amsterdam island." *Journal of Mammalogy*, 74(3) (1993).

Berteaux, D., and T. Micol. "Population studies and reproduction of the feral cattle (Bos taurus) of Amsterdam island, Indian Ocean." *The Zoological Society of London*, 1992.

Bessuges, Jacques. *Le Moine bleu.* Blainville-Sur-Mer: L'Amitié par le livre, 1964.

Bezemer, Henk. *Vier zomers Zeilen.* Baarn: Uitgeverij Hollandia, 1997.

Blond, Georges. *La grand aventure des oceans.* Paris: France Loisirs, 1972–1975 and 1996.

Boorstin, Daniel. *De Ontdekkers (The Discoverers).* Amsterdam: Uitgeverij Agon, 1989.

Cleef, Alfred van. "De verdwenen pakhuizen van Samuel van Cleef." *NRC Handelsblad*, 11 October 1997.

————. "De beloning der rechtvaardigen." *NRC Handelsblad*, 18 October 1997.

Commissaire général (2e S) Ladrange. "Massacre de Marion-Dufresne et de ses compagnons en Nouvelle-Zélande."

Commission Territoriale de Toponymie, avec le concours de Gracie Delépine. *Toponymie des Terres Australes.* Paris, 1973.

Coolhaas, Dr. W. Ph. *Gegevens over Antonio van Diemen.* 1937.

Coudert, Yves. "Le phylica nitida d'Amsterdam." *Revue TAAF*, no. 67 (1976).

Daycard, Laurent. "Situation écologique de l'île Amsterdam—Bilan et avenirs." Académie de Montpellier: Université des Sciences et Techniques du Languedoc, 1985.

Contre-amiral De Brossard. *Kerguelen, le découvreur et ses îles.* Paris: Editions France-Empire, 1971.

Delépine, Gracie. *Les Iles Australes Françaises.* Paris: Éditions Ouest-France, 1995.

Denucé, Jean. *Magellan, La Question des Moluques et la Première Circumnavigation du Globe.* Brussels, 1911.

Dijk, L. C. D. van. "De ontdekking van het eiland (Nieuw-) Amsterdam." *Algemeene Konst- en Letterbode*, 1854.

Floch, Daniel. *Les oubliés de l'île Saint-Paul, des Crozet et des Kerguelen.* Paris: Éditions Ouest-France, 1993.

Guinet, C., P. Jouventin, and J.-Y. Georges. "Long term population of fur seals Arctocephalus gazella and Arctocephalus tropicalis on subantarctic (Crozet) and subtropical (St. Paul and Amsterdam) islands and their possible relationship to El Niño Southern Oscillation." *Antarctic Science* 6, no. 4 (1994).

Henze, Dietmar. "Magelhães, biografie." *Enzyklopädie der Entdecker und Erforscher der Erde.* Graz, 1975 (et seq.).

Holtwijk, Ineke. "Ontberingen en gevaren als het gewone werk." *De Volkskrant,* 7 March 1998.

Jolinon, J. C. *Projet d'Aménagement de l'île Amsterdam.* May 1985.

Jouventin, Pierre. "Past, present and future of Amsterdam Island (Indian Ocean) and its avifauna." *BirdLife Conservation Series,* no. 1 (1994).

————. *Lettre AMAPOF,* no. 30 (September 1991).

Jouventin, P., J. Martinez, and J.-P. Roux. "Breeding biology and current status of the Amsterdam island Albatross Diomedea amsterdamensis." *IBIS,* no. 131 (1989).

Jouventin, Pierre, and Jean-Paul Roux. "Comment un oiseau de plus de trois mètres d'envergure est-il resté longtemps inaperçu?" *La recherche* (February 1984).

Klein, Peter, et al. *Reistogten om den Aardkloot.* Bibliotheek KNAW, 1995.

Koffeman, Niko. "Ortolaan-liefhebber Juppé tart Europa." *De Volkskrant.* 29 January 1997.

Labillardière, M. *Voyage in search of La Pérouse performed by order of The Constituent Assembly during the years 1791, 1792, 1793 and 1794 and drawn up by-.* Translated from the French. London, 1800.

Leupe, P. A. "De Eilanden St Paulus en Amsterdam—Volgens de waarnemingen onzer zeevaarders in de 17e en 18e eeuw." *Verhandelingen en Berigten betrekkelijk het Zeewezen, de Zeevaartkunde, de Hydrographie, de Koloniën en de daarmede in verband staande Wetenschappen.* Amsterdam, 1866.

Marsallon, A. "En 'godonnant' à l'île Amsterdam." *Revue TAAF,* no. 48 (1968).

Martin de Viviès, Paul de. "Il y a dix ans . . . à la Nouvelle-Amsterdam." *Revue TAAF,* no. 12 (1960).

Mercié, M. E. "Aux terres de Kerguelen, îles de Saint-Paul et d'Amsterdam, Récit du périple de l'aviso-transport de la Marine Nationale, L'Eure." *Le Tour du Monde, journal des voyages et des voyageurs,* no. 34 (1897). Reprinted in "Il y a 100 ans: L'Eure," in *Lettre AMAPOF.* February 1993.

Micol, Thierry. "Restaurer la biodiversité—la réhabilitation écologique de l'île Amsterdam." *Pour la Science,* no. 191 (September 1993).

Micol, Thierry, and Pierre Jouventin. "Restoration of Amsterdam Island, South Indian Ocean. Following control of feral cattle." *Biological Conservation*, no. 73 (1995).

Richards, Rhys. "The Maritime Fur Trade: Sealers and Other Residents on St. Paul and Amsterdam Islands." *The Great Circle, Journal of the Australian Association for Maritime History*, April 1984.

Ridderikhoff, Roelff. "Negen maanden racen op de ocean." *De Volkskrant*, 18 September 1997.

Romm, James S. *The Edges of Earth in Ancient Thought*. Princeton, N.J.: Princeton University Press, 1992.

Roux, J.-P. *L'Otarie d'Amsterdam, Actes du VI-colloque de mammalogie*. La Rochelle, 1982.

————. *Sociobiologie de l'otarie Arctocephalus Tropicalis, Thèse spécialité: Biologie des populations et des écosystèmes*, October 1986.

————. "Recolonization Processes in the Subantarctic Fur Seal, Arctocephalus tropicalis, on Amsterdam Island." *NOOAA Technical Report*, NMFS 51 (1987).

Roux, J.-P., P. Jouventin, J.-L. Mougin, J.-C. Stahl, and H. Weimerskirch. "Un nouvel albatros Diomedea amsterdamensis n. sp. découvert sur l'île Amsterdam (37°50'S, 77°35'E). *L'Oiseau et R.F.O.* 53 (1) (1983).

Sigmond, J. P., L. H. Zuiderbaan. *Nederlanders ontdekken Australië, scheepsarcheologische vondsten op het Zuidland*. Amsterdam: De Bataafsche Leeuw, 1993.

South Indian Ocean Pilot, 6th Ed., 1946; 8th ed., 1971; supplement no. 6, 1979.

Traa, Mark. "De puisten van Neptunus." *Trouw*, 20 March 1996.

Valentijn, François. *Oud en Nieuw Oost Indien*. Dordrecht and Amsterdam, 1724–1726.

Vanney, Jean-René. *Histoire des mers australes*. Paris: Librairie Arthème Fayard, 1986.

Vélain, Charles. "Les îles Saint-Paul et Amsterdam." *Annales de géographie*, no. 7 (1893).

————. "Réoccupation par la France des îles Saint-Paul et Amsterdam." *Annales de géographie*, no. 6 (1893).

Zweig, Stefan. *Magellan—Der Mann und seine Tat*. Vienna: Herbert Reichner Verlag, 1937; Fischer Verlag, 1997.

Acknowledgments

The permission for my stay on Amsterdam Island came about through the kind offices of the following people:
J.-P. Kauffmann, Paris; N. Larose-Lont, coordinator of the international desk for the city of Amsterdam; J. Leloup, scientific attaché to the French Embassy, The Hague; M. Lucbert, spokesman for the Minister of Overseas Departments and Territories, Paris; H.A.F.M.O. van Mierlo, Foreign Minister of the Netherlands, and staff members at the Foreign Ministry, The Hague; Ph. Noble, director of Maison des Cartes, Amsterdam; S. Patijn, Mayor of Amsterdam; J.-J. Queyranne, Minister of Overseas Departments and Territories, Paris; H. Wijnaendts, Dutch Ambassador to Paris, and staff member at the Dutch Embassy in Paris.
The following people were of help in my research into old ships' logs and prints: E. Bos-Rietdijk, curator of the Prince Hendrik Martime Museum, Rotterdam, and G. J. D. Wildeman, Maritime Museum, Amsterdam.
Furthermore, I was given advice on biological issues by Yann Tremblay, France, and Bart Van de Vijver, Department of Biology, Universiteit Antwerpen (RUCA); René Kluiving assisted me in interpreting tables of scientific data, and I was given advice on sailing by Henk Bezemer, Amsterdam. Yannick Verdenal helped me on Amsterdam in my search for inscriptions made by castaways.
During the preparation of this book I was advised by: P. Decreau en B. Duboys de Lavigerie of the Association Amicale des Missions Australes et Polaires Françaises, Orléans; G. Penny, ham radio operator, Aalter, Belgium; M. Aimetti, D. Filippi, and J. Sciare, Amsterdam veterans in

Paris; Nathalie Barthoulot corrected the French letters, with which I bombarded the administration of the Southern Lands.

The manuscript was read by Baukje Brugman, Paula van Cleef, Alice van Gorp, Tilly Hermans, Jeroen de Jong, Tanja Lubbers, and René Oey. Jolanda van Gelderen and Mark Hoogervorst helped out with typing during the preparation. Thanks to Margreet Bouwman's Mensendieck therapy and Tonny van der Lee's backrubs, I was able to keep writing.

Finally, my deepest thanks go to Thierry Micol, district chief of Saint-Paul and Amsterdam, the "vacationers," and the members of the 48th and 49th missions on Amsterdam for their help and friendship.

About the Author

ALFRED VAN CLEEF worked for a number of years as a freelance journalist, war correspondent, and producer of radio documentaries. Recently he has authored several books, including *The Lost World of the Berberović Family* and the novel *Longing*.